AdaptAbility

ALSO BY M. J. RYAN

This Year I Will . . .

The Happiness Makeover

Trusting Yourself

The Power of Patience

Attitudes of Gratitude in Love

365 Health and Happiness Boosters

The Fabric of the Future

A Grateful Heart

AS THE EDITOR OF CONARI PRESS

Random Acts of Kindness

More Random Acts of Kindness

Kids' Random Acts of Kindness

The Practice of Kindness

Christian Acts of Kindness

The Community of Kindness

Adapt**Ability**

How to Survive Change
You Didn't Ask For

M. J. Ryan

Broadway Books · New York

Published in the United States by Broadway Books,
an imprint of the Crown Publishing Group,
a division of Random House, Inc., New York.
www.crownpublishing.com

BROADWAY BOOKS and its logo, a letter B bisected on the diagonal,
are trademarks of Random House, Inc.

The author and publisher gratefully acknowledge and credit the
following for the right to reprint material in this book:

Excerpt from Stephen Levine's *Guided Meditations, Explorations and Healings:*
From *Guided Meditations, Explorations and Healings*
by Stephen Levine, © 1991 by Stephen Levine. Used by permission
of Doubleday, a division of Random House, Inc.

Library of Congress Cataloging-in-Publication Data

Ryan, M. J. (Mary Jane), 1952–
Adaptability : how to survive change you didn't ask for / M. J. Ryan.—1st ed.
1. Adaptability (Psychology) I. Title.

BF335.R94 2009
155.2'4—dc22

2009003320

ISBN 978-0-7679-3262-2

PRINTED IN THE UNITED STATES OF AMERICA

Book design by Gretchen Achilles

1   3   5   7   9   10   8   6   4   2

First Edition

Change, when it comes, cracks everything open.

—DOROTHY ALLISON

Contents

AdaptAbility

I.
Welcome to
"Permanent White Water"

It is not the strongest of the species that survives, nor the most intelligent, but the one most responsive to change.

—CHARLES DARWIN

These are challenging times. If you're reading this, chances are you're confronting some change you never asked for—perhaps a loss of job. Or some dream. Maybe you have to learn to work in new ways or find a new place to live. I'm sorry if it's difficult. I'm hoping that within these pages you'll find the support and the practices you need to successfully ride the wave of this change, whatever it may be.

Take comfort that you're not alone. In my work as a "thinking partner," I spend a lot of time speaking to people in all walks of life, from the CEO of a joint venture in Saudi Arabia to a stay-at-home mom who needs to enter the workforce. From where I sit, whether they are searching for a job, looking for funding for a startup, trying to stay relevant at age sixty in a large corporation, dealing with lost savings, coping with a big new job that has one hundred direct reports, struggling to get donations for a nonprofit, or fearing losing their home due to unemployment, people of all ages and walks of life are scrambling to deal with vast changes happening today in every part of the world.

Take the publishing industry, where I've spent thirty years, first as an editor of a weekly newspaper, then as an editor of monthly magazines, a book publisher, and now, for the past seven years, an author. None of the companies I worked for are still in existence. Neither are the distributors. One of my dear friends, a top writer at the *Washington Post,* just took a buyout because the newspaper can't afford to pay top talent—even the most prestigious papers are drowning in red ink. How we create, distribute, market, and promote media products is completely different from even a few years ago. Where it is all heading we truly have no idea. Phil Bronstein, former publisher of the *San Francisco Chronicle,* declared recently, "Anybody who professes to be able to tell you what things will be like in ten years is on some kind of drug."

And that's only one corner of the evolving big picture. In 2006, creativity expert Sir Ken Robinson, speaking at the TED conference (Technology, Entertainment, Design) stated, "We have no idea of what's going to happen in the future. No one has a clue about what the world will be like in even five years."

The only thing any of us can know for certain is that life will continue to change at a rapid pace because the world has gotten more complex and interdependent. Organizational consultant Peter Vail calls this "permanent whitewater," referring to a time of ongoing uncertainty and turbulence. We can't see exactly where these changes are headed or where the submerged rocks are, yet when we're tossed out of the boat, we want to make sure to swim, not sink. Experienced rafters know they're going to get dumped out at some point. The difference between them and the rest of us is that they're prepared to get bounced out and to recover swiftly. They expect the whitewater. And so should we.

Have you ever encountered that "life stress" list that rates changes such as moving, death of a spouse, getting married, etc.? The folks who created that list in the 'sixties estimate that life is 44 percent more stressful now than it was fifty years ago, and they came up with that estimate—I have no idea how—*before* the 2008 global meltdown. I'm not sure we even want to know the new number!

We find ourselves in uncharted waters. How do you cope with the falloff in business of your tiling company due to the implosion of the housing industry, as an acquaintance was telling me about yesterday? Or what should my twenty-three-year-old client do about not being able to drive to work because she can't afford the gas because she gets paid a pittance at her wonderful social services job? What should my husband's fifty-five-year-old friend do now that his job has been rendered obsolete because people aren't buying CDs anymore thanks to the proliferation of downloadable music? What should a sixty-year-old friend of mine do about being upside down in her house? What should a dentist I know do about the huge debt he's carrying from paying for rehab for his son? Which is the more stable situation—the job that my client has had for fifteen years with a company that has just been sold to a conglomerate and is experiencing a shrinking profit margin, or the opportunity with a start-up with seemingly greater risks and rewards?

When people present me with such dilemmas, I don't pretend to know the answers. I'm not a crystal ball reader. Nor do I understand every industry trend. Or how a given company should be positioning itself. What I do know a lot about and what I can help you to do, too, is to develop the necessary mind-sets and actions to adapt well to whatever changes come your way. Knowing that you need to change, or even wanting to change, isn't enough. Without rewiring your thinking and knowing what actions to take, all you get is wish and want and, often, stuckness. I want to help you *actually develop the ability to adapt,* to get up to speed with the attitudes and skills required to make the changes that life and work require.

Why do I place such emphasis here? Because the ability to adapt is, as far as I can tell, the key indicator of success in these turbulent times. It's the capacity to be flexible and resourceful in the face of ever-changing conditions. To respond in a resilient and productive manner when change is required. Another name for it is *agility.* In a recent McKinsey survey, 89 percent of the more than 1,500 executives surveyed worldwide ranked agility as very or extremely important to their business success. And 91 percent said it has become more important over the past five years.

According to *Webster's, agile* means "the ability to move with an easy grace; having a quick, resourceful and adaptable character." *Webster's* has it a bit wrong, I'd say. I don't think it has anything to do with character. It's just that some of us already know how to adapt easily. The rest of us need to learn—quickly. Otherwise you'll end up spinning your wheels, complaining, or contracting in fear when faced with change.

Aikido masters say that to be successful in life, three kinds of mastery are required: mastery with self, which means understanding our feelings and thoughts and how to regulate and direct them; mastery with others, which means being able to create shared understanding and shared action; and mastery with change, which means having the capacity to adapt easily without losing our center— our values, talents, and sense of purpose. This book is focused on the third, although mastery with change requires a certain amount of mastery with self as well. It is my hope that as you go through the changes life brings your way, aided by what you learn here, you become a Change Master, an expert at riding the monster waves of change.

This mastery begins with understanding the process of AdaptAbility. Conversations with my colleagues Esther Laspisa and Dawna Markova have helped me to understand that the process looks like this:

We do this process naturally when a change is small. Say you're planning to go out to dinner tonight with a friend and she calls at the last minute and cancels. You think to yourself, Well that's out (accept), what else could I do this evening (expand)? Then you go do it (take action).

It's when changes are big, painful, confusing, and/or disruptive of your hopes and dreams, that it's hard to see there is a process at work. Being aware of the process can help us avoid getting stuck along the way, suffering needlessly and using up precious time. For we're not just being asked to adapt these days, but to do it speedily. What differentiates the Change Masters I know from other folks is how quickly they can go through the process—okay, that's

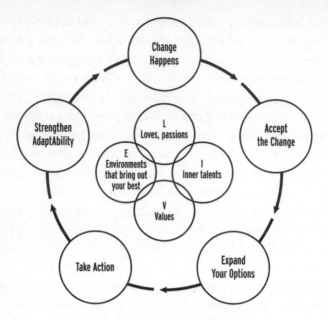

The Process of AdaptAbility

over, now what? They expect to bounce back and are able to see the opportunities that change presents. Fortunately, once you become conscious of how the process of adaptation works, you, too, can face future changes with greater confidence and swiftness rather than getting hung up on the rocks of denial, anger, or helplessness.

Want further incentive to learn AdaptAbility? Experts in mind-body medicine have shown that people who are master adapters live longer and healthier lives than others. How come? Because they counterbalance the stress hormones that wear down our bodies with positive attitudes and behaviors that release feel-good hormones, which restore balance to our cells, organs, and tissue. That's why many health experts define health itself as adaptability. These positive attitudes and behaviors are at the heart of this book.

In order to help you learn to adapt gracefully, I begin with "Seven Truths About Change," which teach you that change is inevitable and explain why it can be such a challenge. The rest of the book takes you through the Adapt-Ability process outlined above—"Accept the Change," "Expand Your Options," "Take Action"—and offers the attitudes and behaviors you need in order to move successfully through each phase. The final section is called "Strengthen Your AdaptAbility," which is a process of noticing what you've learned and recording it so you can use it again when needed—which of course you will because adapting to life is a never-ending process.

You may be at one or another of these phases as you pick up this book. As I always say, do the practices and take the advice that seems most helpful to you. Everyone is distinct, confronting unique challenges, and in need of different support. Whatever you're facing, I want to encourage you to use this book as a life preserver, enabling you to better understand and navigate the changes that change will require in you.

As you go through this journey, you'll learn the following:

- our bodies' physical and emotional reactions to change
- the mental and emotional qualities of a Change Master

- why self-care is crucial
- how to live with uncertainty and to respond in as positive and healthy a way as possible
- how to identify new opportunities
- how to use what's happening to align even more with your talents and values

As with my previous books, this book incorporates insights from brain science, organizational and positive psychology, spirituality, and my own brand of New England pragmatism. In these pages, you'll learn all the tools, techniques, attitudes, and behaviors I know of to be a Change Master. I'll offer many examples from my work with Professional Thinking Partners (PTP), a firm that helps people recognize and develop their unique talents and use them to maximize individual success and collaboration with others. PTP has worked with tens of thousands of individuals in dozens of large and small companies, nonprofits, and governmental agencies around the world. You'll meet PTP's lead consultant Dawna Markova, PhD, who has taught me many of the approaches and techniques you'll find here. And you'll meet many of my clients and friends (in disguised form to protect their confidentiality unless I use their full names), people just like you, dealing with the challenges of life as it is rapidly evolving.

As we face today's realities and try to adapt, it's not surprising that we may need support. Who among us took a class on how to cope with change? In the past, changes happened more slowly and our need to adapt was much, much less. Here's just one example of the acceleration of change.

Starting at AD 1, it took 1,500 years for the amount of information in the world to double. It's now doubling at the rate of once every two years. No wonder we're scrambling to keep up!

What's puzzling about this absence of training in AdaptAbility is that companies all know that their employees' capacity to change is one of the key factors in business success. According to the Strategic Management Research Center, for instance, the failure rate of mergers and acquisitions is as much as 60 to 70 percent. Why? Not because it's not a good idea to bring two organizations together to create efficiencies and synergies, but because the people in them fail to adapt to the changed circumstances. I was just speaking yesterday to a woman in a huge oil company who had been part of an effort to create a standardized process for gathering information across departments. She'd left to work on another project and discovered that, two years and millions of dollars later, the effort had failed. Why? Because employees kept using the old system they knew, rather than learn the new one.

Examples of the lack of ability to change don't have to be that expensive or dramatic. They happen every single day right where you live and work. I would say at least half of the folks I coach on a weekly basis are looking for help adapting to new positions or circumstances where they must drive results in a different way than they have before. The behaviors that have gotten them where they are today are simply not working. And these are all folks who have jobs—those without work need even more support in learning new skills and attitudes.

Resisting change wears down our bodies, taxes our minds, and deflates our spirits. We keep doing the things that have always worked before with depressingly diminishing results. We expend precious energy looking around for someone to blame—ourselves, another person, or the world. We worry obsessively. We get stuck in the past, lost in bitterness or anger. Or we fall into denial—everything's fine, I don't have to do anything different. Or magical thinking—something or someone will come along to rescue me from having to change. We don't want to leave the cozy comfort of the known and familiar for the scary wilderness of that which we've never experienced. And so we rail against it and stay stuck.

When the environment changes and we must therefore, too, it's appropriate to complain—to take, in the words of Dr. Pamela Peeke, the BMW (Bitch, Moan, and Whine) out for a little spin. But soon it's time to put it back in the driveway and get down to business. And that means developing AdaptAbility.

In a very real way, what is being asked of us now is no more or less than to become consciously aligned with what life has always required on this planet. In 1956, the father of stress research, Hans Selye, wrote in his seminal work, *The Stress of Life,* "Life is largely a process of adaptation to the circumstances in which we exist. A perennial give and take has been going on between living matter and its inanimate surroundings, between one living being and another, ever since the dawn of life in the prehistoric oceans. The secret of health and happiness lies in successful adjustment to the ever-changing conditions on this globe; the penalties

TOP TEN CHANGE SINKHOLES

1. getting stuck in denial

2. becoming paralyzed by fear and/or shame

3. spending a lot of time and energy on blame and/or regret

4. believing there is nothing you can do

5. focusing on the problem, rather than the solution

6. using only solutions that have worked in the past to solve new problems

7. "Yes, but"ing all options

8. not getting in touch with what gives you meaning and purpose

9. going it alone

10. resisting or refusing to learn new things because it takes extra effort

Don't worry. In this book, you'll learn how to avoid these danger zones and stay positively focused and moving forward.

for failure in this great process of adaptation are disease and unhappiness."

My goal is to offer you a way to relate to the change you're facing with the least wear and tear and the greatest potential not merely to survive, but to thrive during the greatest period of transformation humans have ever experienced. We are all being called on to stretch mentally, emotionally, and spiritually into the future. It's my hope that this book offers you both comfort and practical support as you take on this challenge, and may what you learn here help you become a Change Master.

II.
Seven Truths About Change

Since we live in a changing universe, why do [humans] oppose change? . . . If a rock is in the way, the root of the tree will change its direction. . . . Even a rat will change its tactics to get a piece of cheese. —MELVIN B. TOLSON

Here you learn the fundamentals of AdaptAbility that will hold you in good stead no matter what wave is heading your way. These understandings will allow you to accept the need to adapt and learn how to get your brain on your side (or, more accurately, the two parts of your brain which are involved in change). With these truths in your hip pocket, you are well on your way toward being able to surf the monster waves of change.

CHANGE TRUTH #1:
Change Is the One Thing You Can Count On

Only in growth . . . and change, paradoxically enough, is true security to be found. —ANNE MORROW LINDBERGH

Christopher Hildreth owns a business installing high-end wood flooring. During the refinancing boom in this decade, his business grew to $4 million. As the economy has slowed, demand for his products has shrunk. Competitors are offering much lower prices and customers have less spare cash to choose the high-end option—if they can afford new floors at all. This development has taken him totally by surprise. In an interview in the *San Francisco Chronicle,* he says, "[I] figured it would just roll along and I would do my estimates and the phone would ring. . . . I would have thought that by now I'd be riding the crest of a wave."

Contrast that response to my client Al's. When I asked him, the CEO of a real estate development company in Las Vegas, how he was doing in the downturn, he confided, "I knew the real estate boom couldn't go on forever. So I created a rainy day fund. I'm not only using it to tide me over, but to buy out troubled developers around town."

Smart man, Al. He knows intuitively there is only one sure thing in life—that things will change. How and when none of us know. But that everything will is absolutely guaranteed. The Buddha called this awareness the First Noble Truth—the fact that everything in life is impermanent. Fighting against that truth only causes us suffering, he taught, because it's fighting against reality. Accepting that truth diminishes our suffering because we're in alignment with the way life is. When we accept that the only thing constant is change, we aren't so taken by surprise when the change occurs. Night follows day, winter follows summer, the moon waxes and wanes. Change happens.

I empathize with Christopher Hildreth because I, too, learned this lesson the hard way. Riding the wave of a couple of bestsellers as a book publisher, I kept expanding my company and had just bought a big new house when the largest returns in the industry rolled back through my door, leaving a deficit the company never could recover from. No matter how many predictions of future sales based on past sales we created, they were wrong because the whole industry was going through a game-changing shift. I wish I had planned for the boom not continuing forever. It would have prevented a lot of sleepless nights.

Even though most of us can't know for sure when and how change will hit us, we can at least keep in our awareness the simple fact that it will. And at a more rapid pace

THE ADAPTABILITY ADVANTAGE

"When the company I worked for merged with another," said Miguel, "we suddenly had a new president. Up until then, ours had been run like a family-owned business—very casual—and people were kept on for years out of loyalty. This new person—who was very, very sharp, both in mind and in style—came in, and suddenly we were faced with demands of a very different corporate culture. We were held accountable for our quarterly bottom lines, and were expected to start showing up more at industry events to 'fly the company flag.' Those who saw the waves of change on the horizon in subtle elements like appearance adapted quickly. No more jeans, no more leggings, no more sneakers. Those that sharpened up were the ones that survived the merger. Those that didn't, like one guy who scoffed at the idea of having to wear a tie, got lost in the flood."

than ever before in human history. Our work and personal lives will change—guaranteed—and we need to be ready with the appropriate attitudes and actions so that, like Al, we minimize the negative impacts and capitalize on the opportunities. When we are aware of change, we can see the signs earlier, so we're ahead of the wave. This gives us a distinct advantage in responding.

CHANGE TRUTH #2:
It's Not Personal

When I hear somebody sigh, "Life is hard," I am always tempted to ask, "Compared to what?" —SYDNEY J. HARRIS

My phone rang. It was a well-known speaker and author asking to work with me. Let's call him Sam. "I've noticed over the last few years," he said, "that things are changing. My speaking fees are beginning to go down and my book sales are, too. Fewer people are attending workshops. There are shifts happening and I need to reposition myself in relationship to them to continue to make a living. Will you help me think that through?"

Instantly I said yes. Because Sam understood something crucial about change which will help him not waste time or precious emotional energy: it's not personal. He didn't blame himself for what was happening. He just observed it and realized he needed to respond in a new way.

What's happening right now to most of us is not because we're bad or wrong or incompetent. It's because the world is transforming at breakneck speed and each and every one of us must adapt to those changes as quickly and efficiently as possible. No one's exempt. Age doesn't get you off the hook (Sam is in his sixties, but you don't hear him complaining that he "should" be able to coast on his laurels until retirement). Nor does how hard you've worked until now, or what your expectations of your life have been. Or what you've sacrificed for or invested in. That's because what's going on has nothing to do with you personally!

Depersonalizing the change challenge you're facing gets you out of a sense of failure and frees up your thinking to be as adaptive as possible, like Sam. I remember the day I learned this. I went to hear Meg Wheatley, author of *Leadership and the New Science.* She's an expert at taking what is understood from the world of quantum physics and ecology and applying it to business. She's no flake— one of her major clients was the U.S. military. She was speaking about the fact that we're still stuck in a mechanistic model of the universe where we think we can make five-year plans for ourselves and our organizations, which is completely out of touch with the way living systems actually work. What I recall her saying was something like, "The way life happens is that things bump up against one another in an information-rich environment and change occurs. Some things thrive and others die out. Think of an aquarium with a bunch of fish. They're all doing fine. Then you put something different in there and it changes the whole ecosystem. Some fish survive, and others die as a result of the new input."

At the time, I was struggling with the financial pressures of my book publishing company and sure I was doing something wrong. I probably was—but all my attention was focused on my "failure," which wasn't helping me come up with new solutions. What Meg helped me do was see that I was just one of the little fish in a big aquarium whose ecosystem was changing.

Once I started viewing it that way, I was able to relate to the situation from a more objective and adaptive frame of mind. As I considered how to respond, it became clear that I wasn't interested in making the changes necessary to survive in the aquarium and so I sold my company. Looking now from the outside at the publishing aquarium, I see even more clearly how what was going on really had nothing to do with me or my efforts.

If the aquarium image doesn't work for you, here's another technique for making the situation less personal. It's called self-distancing. It takes advantage of the brain's ability to make associated images (as if something's happening to you right now) and disassociated images (as if it's happening to someone else). Imagine you are watching a video starring someone else who is going through what you are right now. Give the person in the video a name and see him or her in the situation. Watch what's happening and ask yourself what could be going on that's beyond that person's control or influence. What's your advice for the person in the movie?

A spiritual teacher was once asked her secret to happiness and peace of mind. She replied, "A wholehearted, unrestricted cooperation with the unavoidable." That's what I'm getting at here. It's not so easy—I'm still working on it and don't know many people who do it well. But I do know that the only responsibility we truly have in whatever's going on lies in developing our response-ability to whatever is occurring. As the surfers say, you've got to go with the flow. Otherwise you find yourself under the board faster than you can imagine.

YOU'RE NOT THE ONLY ONE

Resiliency experts have discovered that it's important to see that you're not the only one going through this change. That will help you feel less alone in your pain, which leads to feeling less stress. According to research, a broader perspective on the situation—"It's not just me"—also enabled people to come up with more innovative solutions and better plans of action. So take a look around—you've got plenty of company!

CHANGE TRUTH #3:
Your Thinking Is Not Always Your Friend

With our thoughts we make the world.   —THE DHAMMAPADA

What was the common factor in why people died in Hurricane Katrina? I bet you guessed, as I did and all the media reported, that the answer is poverty. But an analysis by Knight Ridder afterward and reported by *Time* magazine reporter Amanda Ripley in her book *The Unthinkable: Who Survives When Disaster Strikes—and Why* showed something different: the most common factor was age. The older you were, the more likely you were to stay; three-quarters of the dead were over sixty and half, over seventy-five. They had all lived through a major hurricane, Camille, and therefore didn't heed the warnings to leave because they assumed they would make it again. Said the director of the National Hurricane Center, Max Mayfield, "I think Camille killed more people during Katrina than it did in 1969."

The brain is an amazing organ, with incredible social, emotional, conceptual, and linguistic abilities. It can learn from experiences and grow new cells and pathways until you draw your last breath. Neuroscientists are just beginning to understand a fraction of what it can do and how. But not all of what it does is helpful when it comes to responding well to change, as those who stayed during Katrina found out to their peril. Two things in particular stand out from what I've learned about the brain so far.

First, the brain has a tremendous tendency to habituate, meaning to do the same thing over and over. Which is great when you don't want to have to think about how to brush your teeth. But not so good when you need to think creatively about how to cope with a situation you've never been in before. That's why we so often tend to keep doing what we've already done, whether we get good results or not, and are slow to give up some behaviors.

To add to the problem, part of habituation is the brain's tendency to look for patterns, to match current experience with the past—oh, this is just like that thing that happened before. I once read that the average brain generalizes from an example of one, which any good scientist would tell you is not a big enough data pool from which to be drawing useful conclusions. That's what was going on with Hurricane Katrina. The folks who stayed were the ones who'd gone through a massive hurricane before. Their brains said, "This is the same as that." But it wasn't. Environmental degradation, global warming, and sheer bad luck combined to make a change. Younger folks, who never had the experience, heeded the warning because their brains didn't have a pattern to habituate to.

There's an adaptive reason for this habituation. The brain is always on and consumes a disproportionate part of the body's energy. It's only 3 percent of the body's weight yet uses around 20 percent of its oxygen and glucose. It takes less work to be on automatic pilot, so it makes sense from an efficiency standpoint.

When the environment is stable, this autopilot serves us well. But during change, we have to fight against our brain's tendency to look at the situation and see the same old thing, when it's actually encountering something new. The patterns just aren't there to fall back on. We don't know what the stock market is going to do, for instance, despite all the past ups and downs, because we're in a situation that has never occurred before.

Nassim Nicholas Taleb, author of *The Black Swan: The Impact of the Highly Improbable,* says that we previously lived in a country he calls Mediocristan, where cause and effect were closely connected because life was simpler and the range of possible events was small. Now, the global community has entered a country that he names Extremistan, where we are both more interdependent and at the mercy of "the singular, the accidental, the unseen and the unpredicted." (One side benefit of living in Extremistan: it also increases the possibility that one person can make a *positive* difference. Think of Nelson Mandela inspiring the end of apartheid in South Africa or Boris Yeltsin facing down the tanks in Red Square, which toppled the Soviet Union.) Unfortunately, our brains haven't kept up with this new complexity and keep searching for patterns based on the past even when they're not useful.

The other thing to understand about the brain is that we share many of its structures with all mammals (and even reptiles), and therefore it's hardwired to act in ways that were useful when we were being chased by animals in the wilderness but that are not well suited to the complex challenges we face today. This part of our brains, called the amygdala, is constantly scanning for danger but often gives you inaccurate information, sounding the alarm unnecessarily.

You'll be learning about some of the implications of this aspect of our brain structure throughout the book. For now here's just one, as psychologist Rick Hanson and neurologist Rick Mendius put it in an article in *Inquiring Mind.* Because of the advantage there used to be in perceiving danger quickly, "The brain is hard-wired to scan for the bad, and when it inevitably finds negative things, they get stored immediately and made available for rapid recall. In contrast, positive experiences (short of million-dollar moments) are usually registered through standard memory systems, and thus need to be held in conscious awareness for ten to twenty seconds for them to really sink in. In sum, your brain is like Velcro for negative experiences and Teflon for positive ones . . . this built-in bias puts a negative spin on the world and intensifies our stress and reactivity."

In times of change, that's the last thing we need—to perceive what's happening to us as a tsunami when it's only a five-foot wave, to ignore the good and focus solely on the bad. We need to keep perspective so we can be effective in handling the change.

So what are we to do with these tendencies of the brain that don't serve us well during change? We don't have to be solely at their mercy. Becoming aware when we're in one of these habitual thinking ruts is the first step toward making a different choice. Plus, our brain can do much more than these habits and we can use its amazing other capacities to find the solutions we need.

SEE AS IF FOR THE FIRST TIME

To keep from falling into thinking ruts at work, Javier often asks himself, "What if this were a new job in a new company? How would I be behaving? What would I be doing differently? What would I notice that I am now taking for granted? How would I explain this to someone who knows nothing about it?" These questions have helped him keep a fresh perspective and to question what he would otherwise simply accept. Recently it led him to come up with a new marketing idea. If seeing as if for the first time is hard for you, talk to newcomers in your organization. Or to people who are not in the same situation as you. What are they perceiving because they have a "beginner's mind"?

CHANGE TRUTH #4:
Change Isn't the Enemy, Fear Is

Now is the time to understand more, so that we may fear less.
                                              —MARIE CURIE

I met a woman recently who told me a story that really concerned me. Jan's gardening business had dried up, she'd been living on her savings, and she was down to her last $500. One of her clients had called, letting her know of an opening as a receptionist in her husband's office that she knew Jan could fill. "He was looking for someone right away," Jan explained to me, "and I was about to go visit some friends for the holidays. So I told her that I would see if it was still available when I got back next week."

It took all my willpower not to yell, "Are you insane? Unemployment is sky high, you don't have a cent to your name, and you're going to take a vacation rather than a job that's virtually been handed to you?" Fortunately I controlled myself. She'd already made the call so my comment would have only made her feel terrible. But I can't stop thinking about it. What on earth was going on in her head and what lesson is in it for us?

When I asked her how she was feeling about her situation, Jan admitted to being terrified. Fear triggers the fight-or-flight response. Or more accurately the fight, flight, or freeze response. Jan was in flight, avoiding dealing with her situation in a constructive manner. All forms of denial are a flight response.

But flight isn't the only option. In extreme fear, animals, including humans, have been known to literally become paralyzed. At least one of the survivors of the Virginia Tech shootings, for instance, reported that it happened to him. And traders on Wall Street have been known to freeze on the stock exchange floor while watching their clients' money disappear. It's a kind of stupor that creates an unfortunate self-reinforcing feedback loop. The stress hormones that are triggered in the fear response by the amygdala can sometimes increase the fear, making it ever more difficult for the other parts of the brain to respond. If the fear gets strong enough, the amygdala actually cuts off access to the other parts of our brain, and we lose the capacity to think rationally altogether.

Scientists have discovered that you can snap someone out of the stupor that fear can cause with a loud noise, which is why flight attendants, for instance, are now trained to yell at people to get them to move quickly out of a plane in a crash.

The other response to extreme fear is fight—my personal default setting. If I get afraid enough, my anger rises and I look for someone to attack for "making" me feel the way I do. Other people, like Jan, flee—either by literally running away or doing everything they can to avoid dealing with the reality of the change.

So how can knowing this help you? Certainly, not everyone is frightened by change. Some folks are downright exhilarated when everything gets topsy-turvy. Bring it on! they cry. The response depends at least in part on whether you tend to do a lot of innovative thinking or not. (See "What Are Your Inner Talents," page 136.) But for those of us who like predictability and routine, times of great change can bring on intense fear.

That's why it's crucially important to recognize what we're feeling and have coping strategies in place. Fear shrinks our world and limits our ability to think creatively about our choices. It also causes us to isolate ourselves from others who could potentially help and to overgeneralize from this one situation to the feeling that the sky is falling. As we go along, I'll offer specific techniques to avoid—or at least minimize—the fight, flight, or freeze of fear and to increase our ability to accept the situation, expand our options, and make the necessary adjustments.

REMEMBER YOUR ACCOMPLISHMENTS

Whether this is the first time you've ever faced a big change or have encountered challenges before, to help you stay out of fear, list right now the things you've accomplished in your life so far. This will remind you that you're capable of dealing with this challenge as well. Whatever comes to your mind is fine. Here's mine: I built a business from scratch, I lived on $300 a month when I was in my twenties, I've supported myself and my family for the past fifteen years, I've traveled alone around the world, I've spoken in front of a thousand people. Every time you find yourself becoming afraid, remind yourself of your accomplishments, for example, "I put myself through college, I've raised a great son. I can handle this, too."

I know it's possible. I'm one of those who has been in-timidated, rather than exhilarated, by change. I'm happy to report that over the past decade or so, I have made progress on embracing change, which I've come to see is really all about befriending my fear. For my fiftieth birthday, in fact, when former employees of mine at Conari Press wrote a poster called *Fifty Things We Learned from M. J. Ryan*, one of the fifty lessons was "Change is positive." I was floored. I'm not sure if I truly taught them that, but it's certainly a lesson I strive to learn.

Let's face it—change isn't always positive. But fear is the true challenge of change. Our response to even difficult change will be easier when we learn to relate effectively to any fear that arises.

CHANGE TRUTH #5:
There's a Predictable Emotional Cycle to Change

> Change represents the end of your old self. You can look
> back, but you can't *go* back.   —ROBERT HELLENGA

"I can't believe this is happening to me," said the CEO on the other end of my phone line. "They just offered me a contract extension and three months later they're telling me I'm fired. I'm in shock."

Whether you are experiencing a reorganization in your company or bad news in your personal life, change not of your choosing often sets off an emotional process that experts say follows a predictable cycle. Not surprisingly, this cycle is similar to Elisabeth Kübler-Ross's five stages of grief: denial ("This can't be happening to me"); anger ("How dare this happen, it's not fair"); bargaining ("I'll do anything not to have to go through this"); depression ("Why try?"); and acceptance ("It's happening and I can handle it"). That's because unasked-for change always represents a death of some sort—the death of homeownership, for instance, or the dream of parenthood or of an early retirement. It is the death of your expectations for the future. That's why Anatole France said, "All changes . . . have their melancholy; for what we leave behind us is a part of ourselves; we must die to one life before we can enter another."

Whatever you're going through right now and whatever this change means to you, there's always a sense of loss of control. With change that comes from the outside, we aren't in charge of what's happening, and that is very uncomfortable, to say the least. Change experts Ann Salerno and Lillie Brock understand this truth. In their book *The Change Cycle* they note that any change creates "change pain." People are "sad, mad, angry, blaming, afraid," which often drives them "into uncharted emotional waters." Like Kübler-Ross, they describe a movement from shock through difficult negative feelings and ultimately to acceptance and integration. The process may not be linear or swift. You may circle back around to a stage you thought you passed, and it may take longer than you might guess or wish. But ultimately the journey is one of reconciliation with what is and the growth of new possibilities.

What's important to understand here is that there is a

natural trajectory in unasked-for change that is character-
ized by particular feelings. That way you can take some
comfort in the fact that what you are feeling is normal and
that it does have a positive progression, even if you never
come to appreciate the change itself. When you understand that what you are experiencing is grief, you can be
gentle with yourself as you go through the process. If you
suddenly lost a loved one, would you expect yourself to be
forging ahead at the top of your game? You'd be aware that
you're suffering a loss and make sure to treat yourself
kindly.

According to resiliency research, Change Masters allow
themselves to feel their difficult feelings, but they don't
take them on as a permanent state. The section "Accept the
Change" offers a number of practices for dealing with
your difficult feelings while adapting and adjusting to the
new reality. As psychiatrist Steven Wolin points out on
www.psychologytoday.com, it is "possible to be hurt and
rebound at the same time. We human beings are complex
enough psychologically to accommodate the two."

What about my client, the CEO? It's several months
later now. He's gone through denial and anger, and is moving from bargaining and depression to acceptance as he
begins to receive nibbles regarding a new job and to experience the benefits of not working a hundred hours a week
anymore. "I've got time for my daughter, finally," he exclaimed the other day, "and to do some things I love that I
haven't had a chance to do for the past five years." At some
point you, too, will discover a light at the end of the
change tunnel.

CULTIVATE BOTH/AND THINKING

It's possible to both feel bad and move on. It requires that we practice both/and thinking, rather than either/or: "Yes, I feel terrible about losing my house *and* I can make where I'm renting as pleasant as possible"; "Yes, I made financial mistakes *and* I'm still a responsible person." Cultivating the ability to hold both beliefs helps us to experience our feelings *and* rebound, and is one of the foundations of wisdom. Life—and our self—is just too complex for us to get trapped in either/or. So whenever you catch yourself thinking *either this or that*, challenge yourself to think *both/and*.

CHANGE TRUTH # 6:
You're More Resilient Than You May Think

She'd never considered herself to be the kind of person who was cool in the face of crisis—and yet, you never knew what you are capable of until you arrived at that given moment. Life was just a whole string of spots where you continued to surprise yourself.   —JODI PICOULT

"I can't handle this," Susan cried about her daughter's dwindling college fund. I know how she feels. When I think of the changes I've had to deal with in my life— having to lie flat in bed for a year due to back pain, going through a devastating breakup, dealing with the financial meltdown of my company, not to mention all the ups and downs of the life of an entrepreneur—there have been many times when I honestly doubted my ability to live through another second. And yet here I am, and so are you. As the philosopher William James pointed out, "Great emergencies and crises show us how much greater our vital resources are than we had supposed."

We're all survivors of our own lives. You've dealt with changes you never anticipated or wanted and despite your best efforts there are no guarantees you won't have to keep on doing it. (A friend of mine has had *his* house burn down twice, proving that life is definitely not fair.) Despite it all, you're still here! You've made it so far, and that's pretty good evidence that you will continue to, even if some days you don't know how. You and I both have resilience.

According to the American Psychological Association, "Resilience is the human ability to adapt in the face of tragedy, trauma, adversity, hardship, and ongoing significant life stressors." It used to be believed that resilience was something certain folks had and others didn't. Studies of recent events such as 9/11 and soldiers returning from Iraq has revealed that resilience is actually quite common.

It isn't just experts who underestimate our survival capacity. We're all stronger than we give ourselves credit for. I'd been married for fourteen years when, out of the blue, my husband, who was also my business partner, announced our relationship was over. I honestly believed I could not survive emotionally or financially. But here I am, seventeen years later, thriving in a different career and marriage, infinitely more confident in my ability to take care of myself.

That's the amazing thing about change. Some of us do everything to avoid it. We doubt our capacity to live through it. Yet when it arrives on our doorstep, most of us are able to reach deep into ourselves and find the inner strength to strap on a sturdy pair of shoes and walk toward the light.

Research by psychology professors Richard G. Tedeschi and Lawrence Calhoun shows that not only do we have the ability to grow through the challenges of our life, what they call posttraumatic growth, but the benefits of doing so include improved relationships, new possibilities for our lives, a greater appreciation for life, a greater sense of personal strength, and spiritual development. Not bad rewards, I'd say.

So how do we cultivate resilience? Psychology professor George Bonanno of Columbia University and other resiliency experts say it comes from a commitment to finding meaning in what's happening to you, a belief in your capacity to create a positive outcome, the willingness to grow, and the choice to laugh and be grateful.

When I work with myself or someone else who's going through a change they are struggling with, I always ask two questions, the first being, what could possibly be right about this? That helps us to find meaning and to grow. Positive psychologists call it creative construing, the ability to assign a meaning to what we're going through that pulls us into the future in a positive way.

The other question I always ask is, what in your life or yourself can you be grateful for right now? As an author of books on gratitude, I've been awed by its power to uplift and focus us on what is still right, good, and whole in our lives.

The other day, I was introduced via mail to a seventeen-year-old named Lauren. Lauren has lived in twelve different foster homes since she was eight. When she moves from place to place, her possessions fit in one plastic trash bag. She's about to "age out" of the California foster system, with no place to live, no money, no job. But she's happy nonetheless. Because when she was ten, she lived with Mommy Jean. Mommy Jean gave Lauren a rock and told her to carry it always in her pocket. Each time she felt it, she was to think of something she was grateful for. Every day since, no matter where she lives, Lauren's been touching that rock and finding things to be grateful for.

The man who shared Lauren's story sent me a small rock for my pocket. If I could, I would hand one to you right now—not only to help you practice gratitude but to remind you that, like Lauren, you can survive the changes life hurls your way.

CHANGE TRUTH #7:
Your Future Is Built on a Bedrock
That Is Unchanging

Through anger, losses, ambition, ignorance, ennui, what you are picks its way.   —WALT WHITMAN

Tom Heuerman is an organizational consultant who knows a bit about change from both a business and a personal point of view—he writes openly about the lessons he's learned from recovering from alcoholism. Recently he wrote about the qualities of sustainable organizations: they "continually adapt to the external environment . . . [and] have a core identity of purpose (why they exist) and values (guiding principles) that provide stability and continuity as all else changes over time."

What struck me is how much what applies to organizations also applies to individuals. AdaptAbility occurs from the same unchanging bedrock.

Perhaps bedrock is not the only apt metaphor. Biologists know that one of the qualities of a living system is that it is able to respond and adapt to change without losing its basic integrity. Take a cell, for instance. It has a semipermeable membrane that allows things to flow in and out, while maintaining its "cellness."

So it is with you. There is a "youness" that is unchanged, what Walt Whitman refers to as "what you are." A core that will remain no matter how much and how well you adapt. To understand this, it helps to differentiate between who you are as a person and your behavior. To adapt, your behaviors might need to change, but your essence as a person remains the same.

During change, getting more in touch with that "youness" is crucial because it's the raw material you bring to any and all circumstances. Among other things, that "youness," as I've learned from Dawna, is made of four elements: what you love to do, the unique ways of thinking you are excellent at that which you've been doing your whole life, what deeply matters to you, and the environments that bring out the best in you. Together, these create your sense of purpose. How you express these, where you aim them, and how you understand them can and does develop and change over time. But there's some persistent essence, a steady ground note like the beat of your heart. It's why wherever you go, there you are, as Jon Kabat-Zinn famously said.

Take me, for instance. When I knew I had to leave publishing, Dawna, who was one of my authors, invited me to join her consulting company. I had to learn lots of new skills, like leading groups and the principles of an asset focus, which is the underlying basis of the company's work. What I brought with me that was unchanging was my love of reading, writing, talking, and thinking; my combination of analysis and ability to foster the growth of other people; as well as my belief in the ability of people to change; and my tendency to do my best in an environment that offers both time alone and with others. These were the raw materials I had offered authors and staff as an editor and publisher of a self-help publishing company. Now I was simply aiming them in a new direction.

So it is for you, too. You bring with you what you love, your dominant ways of thinking, your values, and the environments that bring out the best in you as you face a change in your life. In the "Expand Your Options" section you'll have a chance to bring these four elements to the surface of your awareness. They are what you can count on no matter what else changes. (See the chapter "Don't Go into the Wilderness Without Your Compass," page 132.)

Here's why understanding these four things is so important. Dawna often talks about her grandmother. One time, when life was asking a big change of me and I was despairing of my ability to cope with it, she told me the following story: Her grandmother was a Jew living in a

Russian village. Throughout the centuries, every so often, the Cossacks would blow through and destroy all the houses of Jews in the village. All you could do, Grandma said, was to hide until they left, then pick through the rubble searching for the whole bricks and build again. Our loves, talents, values, and preferred environments are the whole bricks from which we rebuild.

III.
The Actions of a
Change Master

STEP 1: ACCEPT THE CHANGE

We cannot change anything unless we accept it. Condemnation does not liberate, it oppresses. —CARL JUNG

Whenever we're in a situation that's changing, no matter what it is, the most common initial reaction is—you guessed it—denial, followed by anger. Almost immediately many of us respond to unwanted change with a knee-jerk refusal to accept what's happening, or we rail against having to confront it, uttering (verbally or mentally) refrains like:

"It's not my responsibility."

"I don't have the energy."

"I don't have the time."

"I don't want to."

"This isn't fair."

"This isn't what I signed up for."

"I shouldn't have to. It wasn't supposed to be like this."

Sound familiar? Underneath all those messages is a plaintive cry: I don't know how to adapt and I'm upset that I have to! These thoughts and the emotions underneath are natural, but counterproductive. They trip us up and keep us stuck.

Really, the best first thing we can do rather than stick our heads in the sand is get clear on what is actually happening so we can get down to the business of dealing with it. The acceptance phase is usually the hardest one, since what's happening to us can trigger old wounds and/or require us to go into overdrive in an arena where we'd been happily coasting on autopilot. But it's also the most important one, because if we don't accept the reality of what's happening and deal effectively with our feelings, we simply can't respond in the most productive manner.

That's why this section includes a number of chapters to help you gather the facts. You'll learn why, because of how our brains are structured, gathering information is not as simple as it sounds. Then I offer chapters to help you avoid spending precious energy on denial, blame, shame, or debilitating fear and give you tools to deal with your difficult feelings. My goal is for you to end this section with a more relaxed, less panicked awareness of the situation and a greater ability to respond to it from a centered and clear-minded place. From there, you'll be ready to go into the next phase of brainstorming solutions.

Gather the Facts Like a Newspaper Reporter

> Acceptance is not submission; it is acknowledgment of the facts of a situation. Then deciding what you're going to do about it. —KATHLEEN CASEY THEISEN

I've had a fascinating experience over the past eight years. I've been the thinking partner to several people on the same team at the same time. One effect of this is that I really trust myself when it comes to confidentiality because I don't tell one person what I've heard from another. But another consequence is that I have come to truly see that we're all making up our own reality all the time. One person tells me the meeting was great; another, that it was a disaster. "He's undermining everyone," says one. "He's doing a great job of supporting people," says another. Sometimes I want to ask, "Do you even exist on the same planet?" What I've come to understand is that the answer is no. We each exist on our own planet with its own rules, assumptions, and conclusions, most of which we created so long ago that we're not even consciously aware of them. We're not seeing life as it is, but as we conclude it to be.

This can be very dangerous, particularly in times of change, when being in touch with current reality is very important. How can you ride the wave of change if you don't even have an accurate picture of what direction it's coming from or at what speed? That's why, as soon as you become aware of a change you need to respond to, the very first thing you need to do is get the facts. This may seem obvious, but actually it is not as straightforward as it may seem. First, the situation may be very complex and it may not be clear what the facts are. Exactly what is changing may indeed be hard to determine.

But there's a deeper reason that the fact-finding proposition is so important and challenging. It has to do with how the brain works. To avoid information overload, our brain filters out a great deal of data in any situation and pays attention only to some of it. Then, quicker than you are consciously aware, it takes that data and makes meaning of it. Organizational theorist Chris Argyris calls this process the Ladder of Inference: at the bottom of the lad-

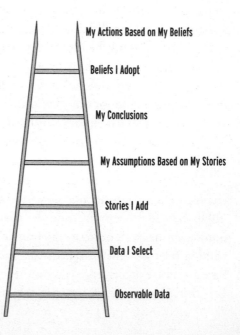

My Actions Based on My Beliefs

Beliefs I Adopt

My Conclusions

My Assumptions Based on My Stories

Stories I Add

Data I Select

Observable Data

der is all the observable data; one rung up, the data I select; then stories I add; my assumptions based on my stories; my conclusions; my beliefs based on my conclusions; and actions I take based on my beliefs. The higher up the ladder you are, the more rigid is your thinking—and the more unsafe you are because you are farthest away from the facts.

Interestingly, although Argyris developed this model decades ago, it seems to fit with a theory by Jeff Hawkins, author of *On Intelligence,* about the structure of the neocortex, the part of our brains that serves as the center of mental function. He believes there are layers—the ones closest to the brain stem take in information and are constantly being changed by incoming data, the ones farthest away have created beliefs about reality based on past experience and kick out all facts that don't fit the frame they've already created, and the ones in the middle try to mediate between the never changing and the always changing.

What's important about this regarding change is to understand that our minds instantly jump to stories, assumptions, conclusions, and beliefs, which can be dangerous if we get caught up in our interpretation of the situation and lose touch with the facts themselves.

You can begin to become aware of your mind doing this by noticing what habitual stories you tell yourself in times of change. Here's mine: let's say a client cancels a day-long training due to budget tightening. Instantly my mind leaps to, "I'm going to end up a bag lady on the street," which, not surprisingly, sends me into panic. Welcome to the contents of my mind.

Your mind may do similarly unhelpful things—

perhaps something like, "I knew this would happen because he's a manager and managers can't be trusted." Or, "It's all my fault because I am worthless." Or, "This shouldn't be happening because I deserve better." As soon as our minds do their jumping up the ladder, we start reacting from our assumptions rather than the facts. In my case, I am now in a panic, a most unhelpful and in this case unnecessary state of mind, since the facts are that it's only one day that's been canceled and I have other business.

That's why, as soon as you become aware that a wave of change is coming your way, the first thing to do is get down to the bottom of the ladder. It's more stable there. That means getting all the facts you can about the situation and resisting the impulse to jump to assumptions or conclusions. Take a tip from Sir Arthur Conan Doyle: "It is a capital mistake to theorize before one has data. Insensibly one begins to twist facts to suit theories, instead of theories to suit facts." Often the facts aren't as bad as our stories about them. And even if they are, once we know the truth of the situation, we can more effectively respond to it.

Tim Gallwey, author of *The Inner Game of Work,* has developed a great set of questions for gathering the facts of current reality which I've adapted here. I suggest that you sit quietly and write down your answers (or ask someone to quiz you), acting as if you were a newspaper reporter—just the facts without any conclusions.

You don't necessarily have to answer all the questions. Depending on your situation, some will be more relevant and helpful than others. The point is to gather as much factual information as you can.

- What's happening? *(I'm spending more than I'm making. I've been using my home equity line of credit to make up shortfalls between my income and expenses.)*

- What do you and don't you understand about the situation? *(I haven't looked at what the gap number is and where my money is actually going.)*

- Do you need more information before taking action? *(I need the facts before I make a plan.)*

- What have you been trying to control here? *(I've been trying to control the situation by not eating out, but that's not making a big enough difference.)*

- What is beyond your control? *(The fact that I can't tap my equity line of credit anymore.)*

- What could you control right now that would make a difference in how you're feeling and/or your situation? *(I can get the numbers and brainstorm ways to tighten my belt. I can work out so I feel at my best.)*

For added help in getting clear about where you are, also consider these bonus questions from author Mark Nepo:

- What keeps coming up, though you keep putting it down? *(I keep thinking I should sell the motor home, even though I don't want to.)*

- What are you needing to attend [to] but don't know how? *(I need to talk to my children about what's going on in a way that doesn't scare them. I saw a good article on that.)*

Now that you've done your investigation, you should have a clearer understanding of the facts of your situation and perhaps an idea of how to begin to move forward.

Acknowledging the plain truth is the first step in acceptance. It doesn't mean you have to like what's happening, simply that you acknowledge reality. And, as spiritual teacher Byron Katie likes to say, it's no use arguing with reality because it wins every time.

HOW HAVE YOU CONTRIBUTED TO THE SITUATION?

"When Bud lost his job, he immediately couched it—for everyone else and for himself—as 'I got laid off,' " explains his wife, Mary. "But the truth is, he got fired. Yes, his firm did eventually lose some key contracts and downsize, but the reason he was the first to be let go was because he'd been told again and again that he wasn't working fast enough. He's very methodical and meticulous, which works brilliantly in certain industries, but not in the sports business, which is very fast paced. He was stubborn, refusing to even consider finding ways to move things along more expeditiously. I always wonder if he would have recovered quicker if he'd been able to actually admit what happened, rather than getting stuck in victimhood for nearly five years." Don't pull a Bud. How have you contributed to the situation? What about feedback you've had from others—is there a grain of truth there? You're strong enough to face the facts and learn for the future. The truth can set you free.

What Other Information Do You Need?

Knowledge is power.
—SIR FRANCIS BACON

Fred walked into the kitchen and told Brigitte, "I'm sorry, but we're going to have to sell this house, and if we can't, we're going to lose it. There's nothing else we can do." Brigitte burst into tears. This couldn't be possible. This was her dream house that they worked so hard for. She had no idea there was a problem. How could this be happening? She was not going to stand for it. They began to fight and Fred ended up storming out of the house.

This scenario played out between a couple, but the underlying dynamics happen all the time in businesses large as well as small, particularly in layoffs and restructurings. Some folks have more information than others. The ones in the know have been thinking through options and scenarios for awhile. During that time, they may even be telling the other people involved that "everything's fine." Then they come out with a fait accompli, leaving the people receiving the message to feel broadsided or even deceived.

If you're on the Fred side of the story and haven't announced a change yet, consider giving the people involved a heads-up. That's what the nonprofit my brother-in-law works for did. They said there might be layoffs in three months depending on donations. That allowed my sister and him to prepare, emotionally and financially. When you give the heads-up early on, you also allow for the possibility that others may bring creative ideas to the situation that you hadn't considered. For instance, maybe your staff is willing to take reduced hours or a two-week unpaid vacation so that no one needs to be laid off.

You also create more buy in when you involve people in thinking the situation through. Maybe Brigitte would have been more willing to give up the house if she'd been part of the conversation earlier on. At the very least, when you announce a required change, be sure to offer a context for your decision—what you thought of and why you came to the conclusions you did—so the others have a chance to get up to speed.

If you are on the Brigitte side, you may have no choice about how or when you receive the news. But you can be aware that understanding the causes and the need for change may help you cope better. You may never agree with the decision, but when you understand what caused the Freds of the world to make the choice they did, it may make acceptance a bit easier.

If this is a change that you've been hit with by someone else, here are some questions you may want to ask in order to understand what's going on as fully as possible. They may seem basic, but given that change can trigger your fight-or-flight response, which cuts down on your capacity to think logically, a cheat sheet to help gather the facts might be useful. In parentheses are possible answers in two scenarios—a layoff and a house loss—to give you a sense of how it might go.

- What's changing? (*We are shutting down the business./ We need to sell our home and move.*)

- What factors led up to the change or what events drove the change? *(Customer demand is down due to the economy./The value of our house has dropped below the amount of our mortgage.)*

- What specific events/actions are going to occur? *(Everyone will be laid off./We need to hire a real estate agent.)*

- When will these events/actions occur? *(You will be terminated on August 1./ASAP.)*

- Who else is impacted by the change? *(All forty-five people will be laid off./We need to talk to the kids.)*

- How was this conclusion reached and what alternatives were considered? *(We tried to get an extension on our line of credit but were turned down./I tried to get a new mortgage, but the drop in value would require us to make a big up-front payment that we cannot afford.)*

- What options are available to deal with the impact on me? *(You should apply for unemployment insurance./We can find something smaller to rent or we can move in with my mother.)*

- What resources are available to help me through the change? *(Being a small company, we don't have outplacement services, so you will have to look for help elsewhere./Real estate agents, online sites.)*

- How are others in a similar situation dealing with this? *(Perhaps you can create a support group with the other employees./Let's call the Gonzaleses; they went through this.)*

As for Fred and Brigitte, when Fred realized that he hadn't let his wife in on his reasoning, he went back to square one. He presented the problem and asked her to think with him about a solution. In the end, she came to the same conclusion as he had and they sold their house. But this time they were on the same page.

The Truth Will Set You Free
(Or at Least into Motion)

Denial ain't a river in Egypt.
—ANONYMOUS

Sandra was slowly sinking into debt each month. Her graphics business was just not making enough money. Periodically she'd get her eighty-three-year-old mother to give her a loan, which she'd never pay back. When family members would ask about it, she'd say, "I'm a fifty-nine-year-old woman. I'm doing all I can. There's nothing else I can do."

One day, her sister and daughter decided to intervene. They sat her down and said, "You have a problem. You can't go on like this. We're here to help." First they went over her budget with her. Sandra hadn't looked at the figures in more than a year. "We helped her see the actual amount of money she was losing each month and brainstorm ideas of how to make it up," explained her sister. "When she said, 'There's nothing else I can do,' we went on Craigslist with her to see what jobs were available and what the requirements were. She realized that she did have the ability to do many jobs listed there. She's since gone out and gotten a part-time job that enables her to keep her business running and not go in the hole."

Denial can take many forms. It can be a refusal to admit there's a problem, or an inability to look squarely at the situation, or to take action on it. Or it can be certainty that attempts to make the situation better are futile: "Why try? It won't make a difference." Deep down, we're afraid the problem is too big or hairy to cope with. So we ignore that it's there. If we know it will mean giving up something we're strongly attached to or even addicted to, we may pretend it's not going on so we won't have to do the painful work of change.

As people who love those with addictions know, you can't make someone come out of denial. How and when a person decides to confront reality and change remains a mystery. Interventions often work, however, because they can wake the person up out of the trance she's been in—she may see that the situation is serious enough that you've gathered together to talk about it. And she may realize she doesn't have to face the change alone—you're going to help.

I'm not suggesting that if you love someone with an addiction that you stage an intervention on your own. That takes real experience and expertise.

But if you're concerned that someone you're close to needs to accept the reality of a situation and just needs a little push to get going, sometimes straight talk, coupled with help in getting them started, can work. An Internet entrepreneur told me the other day of a very useful conversation he had with his accountant. The accountant said, "After looking at your books, I need to tell you it's down to your business or your house. If you don't let the one go, you will lose the other." "It was just what I needed in order to stop hoping for a miracle and go out and look for a job," said Bob.

A friend had been telling me for months she needed to look at her finances because she knew she was spending too much. I offered to sit with her as she faced the music. The numbers showed she was spending $2,000 more a month than she made. Like so many of us, she'd been living off that lovely piggy bank—the equity in her house—which suddenly dried up. Looking at the actual number was the wake-up call she needed to get a serious budget in place and a plan to pay off her huge second mortgage.

No one can "make" anyone else change, as you've most likely already discovered in your life. But we can offer kind truth telling and support to help the people we care about to turn and face reality.

HELPING YOURSELF OUT OF DENIAL

Here are some good questions to ask yourself. If you're in denial, they may help jolt you out. If not, they may help you get into action even quicker:

1. What do you imagine the consequences of not doing anything might be?

2. Given those consequences, what would you tell a close friend to do?

3. Who or what do you need to help you take your advice from question 2?

If You Can See It, It's Yours to Deal With

If we don't change direction soon, we'll end up where we're
going.   —PROFESSOR IRWIN COREY

"They are driving me crazy," said Lily, the owner of a consulting firm. "Business keeps declining and my staff keeps
coming to our meetings having done the same old thing.
Don't they see that they need to be offering customized solutions and marketing our work differently?"

Lily's comments stuck with me because I'd heard them
in various forms three times in one week. These were all
people who wished that others would see a need for change
and take action. What I found myself saying again and
again was, "If you see it, it's yours to deal with. Not everyone is good at reading signs of needed change or coming
up with new ideas. The fact that you are means it's your responsibility to lead the way. Rather than complain that
they can't, how about celebrate that you can? Then do
something about it—help them see what's needed and how
they can offer it."

Human beings have different talents and capacities.
That's one of those truisms that is easy to say and very
hard to live with. Deep in our hearts we don't want that
to be true. Maybe because if it's true, then we have to take
serious responsibility for the talents and capacities we
have. It's scary to realize that if we don't offer our part, the
system—family, business, community organization—
may falter.

In times of change, we can't afford to waste time on

"Why can't they see the building's on fire?" They can't and you can, so it's your job to help them see the situation for what it is and to think with them about all the resources you have to come up with a response. That may mean ideas, training, coaching, or more supervision or input from you.

In Lily's case, she decided that because she was good at coming up with innovative solutions and no one else on her team was, rather than trying to train them to think like her, it was more efficient to look at each proposal before it went out and see if she had something to add or change. Over time, she saw that a couple of people caught on and she was able to have them help the others.

If an employee of yours continues to refuse to acknowledge a need for change despite your support, then perhaps that's a hint that he or she is not the right person for the job. But what if it's a colleague, spouse, or other family member? In other words, a situation where you don't have hiring and firing power? Then you need to think about what actions you can take to address the situation that's not contingent on them. This is usually easier at work than at home. You can begin to look at costs each week, for instance, even if your colleague or boss doesn't.

There are things you can do on your own at home, too. For instance, if you know you need to tighten your belts and your wife doesn't get it, brainstorm a list of things you can do on your own to save money. You may also consider asking for help from a counselor, minister, or friend so the two of you can get on the same page.

What's important to understand is that the acceptance you may need to do in a time of change is accepting that you are the one who perceives it and thus must initiate options and actions. You wouldn't stay in a burning building because no one else saw it was on fire, would you? Sound the alarm and get yourself and others to safety.

How Could This Be Good Luck?

What helps luck is a habit of watching for opportunities, of having a patient, but restless mind . . . and of passing through hard times bravely and cheerfully.

—CHARLES VICTOR CHERBULIEZ

Monroe Mann is an actor, writer, musician, and filmmaker. Years ago, he decided to sign up for the Army National Guard, never dreaming that it would mean that one day he would be deployed to Iraq. Talk about unasked-for change! "I had to break the lease on my Manhattan office, stop preproduction on a film I was gearing up to shoot, and my band broke up as well," he explained. "It was a difficult time. I was not prepared for it. Ironically, it wasn't that I was ill prepared for combat. I was ill prepared to leave all that I had worked so hard for behind. I was really stressed out about what the deployment would mean for my business and my career.

"Then I took a deep breath, stepped back for a moment, and made a list of all the good things that this change would bring me and all the things I was going to do to turn this 'unasked-for change' into an 'unasked-for blessing.' In making the list, I realized that this deployment would make me a cooler person; it would give me great

fodder for screenplays; it would entitle me to many benefits for combat veterans; and it would make me a more
confident and well-traveled person.

"In the end, the deployment resulted in a number of
great successes: I wrote and published a new book while I
was there; I shot seventy-five hours of footage that I am ed-
iting into the world's first comedy documentary about the
war in Iraq; and I even was nominated for a bronze star for
my efforts training the 4th Iraqi Army. Not bad results
from a combat zone!"

Monroe e-mailed me after hearing that I was looking
for stories of unasked-for change. His arrived the day I was
to turn the book in. I hurried to include it because it's such
a great example of how the story you tell yourself about
what's happening can make change either a terrible thing
or a portal to new possibilities.

Especially if this is the first time you're going through a
major setback, it can be a shock to your system. You had always thought you were lucky, that bad luck (divorce or debt,
illness or getting fired) was for other people. What Monroe's
story asks you to consider is that whether a change is bad
luck or good, depends to a great extent on what you make of
it. "Luck" is found through your capacity to see the difficulty
as an opportunity and meet it with enthusiasm.

I'll never forget the day my friend Andy Bryner came to
comfort me in the midst of the searing initial pain of my
divorce. He whispered in my ear, "You don't know it yet
but this breakup is some new guy's lucky day." I found him
six months later. That's when I learned that you can never
assume that unasked-for change isn't a blessing in disguise.

Monroe did two powerful things. First he asked how

this could be good for him and came up with a list of things that were positives in the situation—travel, health benefits, etc. But he didn't stop there. He then asked himself how he could turn a bad situation to his advantage, which is what led him to create a film and write a book. Monroe turned his bad luck into good through his attitude and his actions.

How about you? Accepting what's happening is easier when you look at how this could be good luck, at least down the line, and then, like Monroe, work on making sure that it becomes so. At the very least, remind yourself that this is not the end of the story—you really don't know whether it will be good luck ultimately.

"YOU NEVER KNOW WHEN YOUR BAD LUCK IS YOUR GOOD LUCK"

"I took this job because I was desperate," explains José. "We'd just moved, my wife was out of work, and I got laid off. It was for way less money than my previous job, doing something I wasn't thrilled about. But it turned out to be the best thing for me and my family. My wife is away a lot for her new job and I get to work at home, which gives me great flexibility in picking up the kids or handling some house emergency, like letting the guys in to fix the furnace. I have more vacation time than I've ever had before, actually have time to work out, and have really gotten into cooking. You never know when your bad luck is your good luck."

"Worry Well"

I have been through some terrible things in my life, some of which actually happened. —MARK TWAIN

There's a cartoon I've had over my desk for years. It shows a woman up at a chart with a pointer. The chart has two columns, one huge and one tiny. She's pointing to the big one, saying, "This is everything you've ever worried about. That's everything you've ever worried about that actually happened." I keep it to remind myself of my tendency to catastrophize, to scare myself with all the possible "what ifs" my mind loves to obsess over.

Like Mark Twain, I've lived through terrible things, some of which actually happened. Still, I would prefer not to exist in a state of constant panic over changes that may or may not come my way. Besides making life miserable, it kills brain cells and ages you faster because at high levels cortisol, one of the hormones released in the fight-or-flight response, is toxic to all the tissues in your body. So I've worked for years on strategies for staying out of fight or flight.

Here's how it works. The amygdala is constantly scanning the environment for two things—pain versus pleasure, safety versus danger. It wants pleasure and safety. If it perceives danger or pain, red alert, the stress response gets switched on as the amygdala initiates a call to action—fight, flight, or freeze. Messages from the environment go to both the amygdala and other parts of your brain, but they always get to the amygdala faster. That's why we must get more skillful at learning to interpret the messages. The trick is to use the logical part of your brain to convince the scared part of yourself that there is no danger, at least none that you can't deal with.

That's why I ask my clients when they are going through some change, "What's the worst thing that could happen?" Much of the time they realize it's not that big of a deal: "I'll have to work a few years longer," "She'll have to take out a student loan," "I'll have to live on a budget."

But sometimes, they continue to be scared: "I'll lose my house and end up on the street," "I'll lose my job and never work again," "I'll never see my daughter for the rest of my life." Dawna has taught me that, in these situations, what we're doing is telling ourselves a story of limitation in which we are stuck partway. In those circumstances, what works is a technique she calls "worrying well." It entails taking the story all the way through to the end so you can see that you can survive it.

I've done this many times and it's really helpful. Here's an example. A client of mine is fearful about losing her house. I ask her, "Okay, so you lose it, then what happens?" She thinks for a while and then responds, "I guess I'd go live with my sister." "And then what happens?" "Well, it's hard at first because there's not enough room for all my stuff and that feels bad. As time goes on I realize that because we're pooling our incomes, things aren't as tight and I'm not so stressed out all the time. I really love my sister and have been sad that we live so far apart and rarely see each other. You know, maybe it's not so bad after all."

Asking yourself, "And then what happens?" allows you to access all of your inner and outer resources to come up with a solution you can live with, perhaps even thrive as a result of. You realize there are always options, if only in the way you choose to look at the situation. It doesn't even matter that in reality you may end up doing something different from what you imagined. What's important is that through this process you get in touch with your capacity to go on. You and I are stronger and smarter and more resourceful than we imagine when we're scared. Worrying well helps us find our way through.

GIVE YOURSELF A BREAK

Yes, you should relate to your feelings. But dwelling on your negative thoughts and feelings, it turns out, isn't so good for you. It can help you stay stuck. The more you focus on the negative, the more you grow your tendency to focus on the negative, because the brain cells that fire together wire together, creating an all-too-convenient pathway for your thoughts. So give yourself breaks from thinking about the problem. Walk, dance, see a funny movie, do yoga, go out with a friend and talk about something else. If you feel anxious, note that the latest research reports that a distraction that requires concentration, like chess or Sudoku, is better at preventing worry than a more mindless one like watching TV. Experiment with what works best for you.

What Core Issue Does This Trigger?

The road forks. One path leads to further entanglement, re-activity, and a thickening of the fog of confusion, the other toward the refinement of awareness and the unfolding of compassionate wisdom. The choice is ours in every moment.

—TARA BENNETT-GOLEMAN

Deidre didn't get a large sale for her gourmet-food product line that she was hoping for. "I knew it," she exclaimed, "those people have been out to get me for as long as I've been working with them." Hmm, I thought, that's not how I see it. They'd bought her products for two years, and were now having money troubles and looking to save wherever they could. Why did Deidre interpret it as an attack against her?

As I wrote about earlier, human beings take information and interpret it. It turns out that a great deal of that interpretation comes from one or more core ways of explaining what happens to us that we developed through our early childhood experiences. Our brains create these explanations and then continue to look for them in other situations as a way of keeping us safe. Some psychotherapists call these schemas. In her book *Emotional Alchemy,* Tara Bennett-Goleman identifies ten and describes them as:

Abandonment: "I'll end up alone."

Deprivation: "My needs won't be met."

Subjugation: "It's always your way, not mine."

Mistrust: "They're out to get me."

Unloveability: "I'm not lovable."

Exclusion: "I'm always left out."

Vulnerability: "I'm responsible but can't control the situation, so I feel overwhelmed and worry excessively."

Failure: "I'm not good enough."

Entitlement: "I'm special, so rules don't apply to me."

Perfectionism: "I have to do everything perfectly."

One of mine is Deprivation, so when a change hits me, my first thought is I'll end up starving on the street. Every time. A way to identify these for yourself is by their all-or-nothing quality. From one canceled client I leap to death on the streets. That's a clue. Another is that it somehow keeps happening to you: *Here it is again. No matter what I do, I never feel safe enough.*

When we're acting from a schema, it's like wearing green-tinted glasses that make the world look green and being convinced that it's green in reality. What started out as a way to protect us from further harm ends up causing harm because we aren't necessarily seeing the situation accurately.

Schemas are much easier to see in other people—James is so paranoid, you might think; or Sheila's always going on about how she's so special and she's upset that no one seems to notice. These are signs of their schemas (Mistrust and Entitlement) and likely aren't yours if you notice them. If a person has a similar one to yours, then you interpret what they say as simply confirming reality.

It works the other way, too. Because someone close to you may not share your schema, he or she may have a hard time understanding why you're reacting to the situation the way you are. It doesn't trigger the same thing in them.

Becoming aware of your particular schema is important during change because it allows you to begin to step out of the situation and perceive it more objectively, and therefore respond more effectively. But we're all very invested in believing our schemas, so simply becoming aware of them isn't going to change them. But awareness *is* the first step.

So how do you become more aware? Says Bennett-Goleman, "When you are unusually upset, preoccupied by persistent emotions, or behaving impulsively and inappropriately," that's a clue that a schema is at work. She then suggests that you:

- Acknowledge that one or more schema may have been triggered.

- Notice the feelings in your body (*I feel a fluttering at my heart/a sinking in the pit of my stomach. . . .*).

- Notice your thoughts that go with the sensations (*I'm telling myself I'll end up alone/that I have to be perfect.*).

- Notice your actions based on this belief (*I'm panicking and selling my stocks at an extreme loss./I'm worrying night and day.*).

- Ask what this reminds you of that may be the origin of your schema (*It reminds me of the time when I was little and hungry and my mother was drunk and ig-*

nored me./It reminds me of when my parents divorced and I had to become the man of the family.).

• Challenge the schema by finding evidence against your belief: (*I'm not going to starve—I have money in the bank, friends who will help me./I have been imperfect in the past and people still loved me./I have gotten my way many times—just yesterday my wife asked me which video I wanted to see.*).

This is deep work. What's most important here is to become aware that a schema may be driving your response to the change you're facing and making it especially hard. It may be interfering with your ability to perceive the situation as it really is.

When Debra understood that her schema of Mistrust had been triggered, she asked her business partner to give her other ways of viewing the situation. This helped her respond to her customers in such a way that she ended up with some business instead of none.

Relate to Your Fear

If you're going through hell, keep going.
—WINSTON CHURCHILL

Recently, I got an e-mail from Ted. He's a consultant who has worked with me in the past. He was letting me know that he just lost his biggest client and was wondering if I had work we could do together. He was making the right practical move in such a situation—reaching out and networking with everyone he could think of. I know him well so I decided to call to see how he was doing emotionally.

"I'm okay, I guess," he replied to my question. "I'm trying to stay as busy as possible and not think about what could happen if I don't find work soon. But I do find myself waking up in the middle of the night in a panic. I play the worst-case scenarios over and over in my head and it's hard to go back to sleep."

Ted is like most of us in a challenging situation. We "try" not to be afraid, only to have our fears wake us up. A friend calls it the night wobblies. I know them intimately. When my book publishing company was having financial trouble, when I owned two houses because I bought a new one before selling the old (bad idea in hindsight), I spent countless waking hours trying not to panic as all my fears flooded in.

That's because trying to ignore or deny our fearful feelings doesn't work very well. Nor does trying to talk yourself out of them. Or having someone else try to talk you out of them. (My ex tried that without success for fourteen years with me.) They're still there, below the surface, just waiting for us to stop so they can ambush us. They can come at night or during odd moments of the day.

Either way, as you may have already discovered, a strategy of suppression doesn't work too well. That's because, as I've explained, we've got the logical part of our brain, which tells us we "shouldn't" be afraid, and the limbic system, particularly the amygdala, which triggers fight or flight. Hence the wakefulness at night. When the neocortex is sleeping, the more primitive part of our brain breaks through·with its panic signal, the stress hormones are released, and there you are, staring at the clock.

Whether your situation has you experiencing the night wobblies or feeling anxious, angry, or fearful during the day, there is a better way than panicking, acting out, or trying to suppress your feelings. It involves relating to your fear rather than giving into it or trying to "control" it.

There are a variety of ways to do this, but the one that I've found to work the best is a five-minute meditation called BBLISS created by Dawna. It strengthens the neocortex's ability to intervene during times when the amygdala is kicking into survival mode. You can do it anytime you notice your fear or anger. But because it actually increases the neocortex's ability to be in charge, it's even better if you also do it four set times a day—in connection with meals and/or waking and going to sleep. You can even set an alarm on your BlackBerry as a reminder. The more regularly you do it, the less you'll experience panic, day or night.

B—BODY

Bring your awareness into your body and do a body scan from your feet up to your head. Use your attention as a "flashlight" to scan your body and notice, without judgment or commentary, your feelings and sensations. For instance, "My feet are heavy, my chest is tight, my head feels like it's being gripped in a vise, etc."

B—BREATH

Take three full rounds of breath. Each round should include a full inhale, a pause to notice the space between the inhale and exhale, a full exhale that lets go of what is old, and a pause to notice the space at the end of the exhale. Hang out in the space at the end of the exhale like hanging out in a hammock. Notice how the inhale comes back all by itself.

L—LISTEN OUT

Listen to and notice the sounds around you. Let your hearing become receptive as if you are breathing in and out of your ears.

L—LISTEN IN

We are always telling ourselves stories about our situation. That's one of the things our brains are designed to do—to take in information and then make meaning out of it. Listen to the stories you are telling yourself in the moment. Simply notice them, without judgment.

I—ACKNOWLEDGE THE "I" STORIES

Acknowledge the stories you are telling yourself. "I hear that I am telling myself (fill in your own story in the moment)." For instance, "Oh, I am telling myself that I will never be a mother." Or that "I will always be alone."

S—SENSATIONS

Again, without judgment, notice the sensations that happen in your body as a result of those stories. For instance, "My breathing gets more shallow, my throat gets tight."

S—SENSE

Finally, sense the life force pulsating through you and recognize that you are alive. Name something you are grateful for. Appreciation, as I wrote about earlier, will help you stay out of fight or flight.

Doing BBLISS regularly will help integrate your mind and body. It brings your awareness to both of these aspects of your being, as well as to both inner and outer reality. It helps you get off the train of overwhelming, fearful thoughts and experience what's going on for you in a different way—at the level of sensation and breath rather than story. But it only works if you do it!

Send Out an SOS

I get by with a little help from my friends.
—THE BEATLES

I was a seventeen-year-old senior in high school going through my first heartbreak. I'd received a Dear John letter from the guy I'd been in love with for two years. This was definitely a change I didn't ask for! Without thinking, I jumped into my mother's car and drove about half an hour to the home of two of my teachers. I knew where they lived because they'd had a school gathering there. They weren't home, so I camped out on their doorstep until they returned. They poured tea and sympathy as I poured out my heart. We've been friends ever since.

Following that impulse was one of the smartest things I've ever done. Not just because they helped me get through my heartbreak, not just because of our enduring connection, but because I learned a crucial lesson that has stood me in good stead over the ensuing forty years. When a wave of unwanted change hits, run as fast as you can to get help. From a friend, a colleague, a mentor.

There are three kinds of support other people can give, say social psychologists—tangible support, like money, food, and shelter; advice and help with problem solving; and empathetic listening. Think about which you need most at the moment and who might be able to offer it.

In studies of resilience, it's been shown over and over that people who thrive reach out and ask others for support. They're not afraid of revealing the difficulties they're going through and are good at picking out people to befriend. This is not as difficult as it might appear. Frankly, the reason I drove to these particular teachers' door was that I knew where it was. I'd guess most people you know would be happy to listen. It just requires being brave enough—or upset enough, in my case—to not care if you sound like a fool or a failure. Does someone come to mind? If not, take a risk, like I did, and try with an acquaintance who you guess will be supportive. Chances are you'll feel better. If not, try someone else.

This is one arena where women have an advantage over men. It's recently been discovered that during the stress response, when the hormones are released that create the fight, flight, or freeze response, women secrete another hormone, oxytocin, which gives us another option for how to respond—to bond with others. UCLA social psychologist Shelley Taylor calls it the tend-and-befriend response. Because of this built-in tendency, women more naturally seek out others when times are tough. Men are another story. They tend to try to tough it out alone.

If you need more convincing that revealing yourself and your problems is good for you, consider the results of these three fascinating studies:

Researchers gave two groups of people the task of carrying heavy backpacks up a hill. The individuals in one group had to do it solo; the other, with friends. Before doing the task, each group was asked to rank the difficulty of the task. Guess what? The people alone all ranked the task harder than those who had friends with them.

In a similar study, when people were asked to guess the weight of a box filled with potatoes, those who believed they were going to have help lifting it estimated it to be lighter than those who thought they were going to be alone in the task.

Finally, when folks had to estimate the slope of a hill, they thought it was less steep when they were with others.

HOW FRIENDS CAN HELP

As my friend Kate discovered, friends can help you get out of denial and into action. "About eight months after my marriage ended," she wrote, "I had to move, and the expenses to do so were high. I was scrambling to pull it all together. A friend and I were talking and she asked me if I'd gotten around to getting my engagement ring appraised. It was a big old diamond, worth a lot of money. I said I didn't want to sell it, that I was saving it for an emergency. She said to me: 'Let me get this straight. You're saving it for a rainy day? Honey, it's pouring!' It was all I needed to sell that ring and move."

What this all means is that having someone by your side will help your challenge feel less difficult. Isn't that a boost we could all use about now?

Recognize if You're Milling

Acceptance is not a state of passivity or inaction.
—PETER MCWILLIAMS

Dwight is an entrepreneur who owns a PR company that's struggling. There's a lot he could be doing proactively, he tells me, but instead, he finds himself curiously not doing much of anything—not reaching out to potential clients, not returning phone calls promptly.

I'm hearing similar things from other people; that as they face uncertainty, whether due to a reorganization in a large company or the possibility of a layoff in a small one, just when you think they'd apply their best effort to increase the possibility of success, a slacking off occurs. What's that about? I wondered.

Then I read research by Robyn R. M. Gershon at Columbia which shows that during a disaster, there is a phase where we delay action because we aren't sure whether we need to respond or what the right action might be. We mill around, our pattern-seeking brains trying to gather more data to make a decision.

Milling causes delay. According to a National Institute of Standards and Technology survey, the average time before survivors evacuated at the World Trade Center on 9/11 was six minutes, and some people waited as long as forty-five minutes. Rather than just get out, people first called friends and family. Many even took the time to power down their computers.

In an emergency, who you mill with can mean the difference between life and death. With luck, you'll speak to someone who says, "We need to take action—now."

Even though you may not be in a life-or-death emergency where time is of the essence, it's good to be aware if you are caught in milling that's interfering with your ability to get into action. Do you find yourself slacking off? Pushing projects onto others, not being proactive in meetings, not getting to the important things on your to-do list, taking a week to do what you used to in a day? Or perhaps you are doing what psychologists Salvatore Maddi and Deborah Khoshaba call regressive coping—doing things that are "irrelevant to the task" that result in "some momentary relief but . . . little to remedy the problems."

If you catch yourself in any of these behaviors, ask yourself, "What do I need to get into action? Is it more information? A person to talk to who may have experience and perspective that can help your brain get what it needs to get going?"

A friend, fearful of a layoff, found himself in this state. "Once I realized I was stuck in wasting-time mode, I reached out to a colleague in the finance department who said, 'We always do salary reductions before any layoff and we're not even talking about that yet.' It was all I needed to get back to my desk and pound out the five sales letters I'd been procrastinating on all week."

Rather than beat yourself up for procrastinating or being lazy, understand that milling is a natural human response to crisis. It's a cue for you to figure out what you need ASAP.

It's Good to Bitch and Moan but Not Forever

It is a waste of time to be angry about my disability. One has to get on with life and I haven't done badly. People won't have time for you if you are always angry or complaining.

—STEPHEN HAWKING

Karen is a stay-at-home mom of three kids with a live-in nanny, which is pretty common where she lives. It enables her to take each kid to activities without having to drag all three everywhere she goes, and also affords her a little bit of alone time to get errands done. Her husband has informed her that they have to scale back and the nanny has to go.

Karen is appalled. She refuses to see that there might be any other way to manage her daily life than how she's been doing it all along. She won't consider day care, because no one where she lives "does that." She "can't" manage all three kids on her own without having to make serious sacrifices, and she's not willing to do that. She's furious at her husband, and they are deadlocked. Meanwhile, regardless of how angry Karen is, the nanny is going at the end of the month. Karen needs to make a plan, and fast, but she won't let go of "this isn't fair," the anger stage of the grief process.

As I wrote about earlier, when unasked-for-change hits us, it sets off a series of often downright painful feelings—anger, grief, fear. Our feelings are valid and it's good to express how you're feeling, to bitch and moan, to whine and complain. It's appropriate for a while to let it all hang out.

But after a certain point, we can get trapped in our feelings, which gets in the way of accepting the change and moving forward. Anger hardens into bitterness; depression, into permanent lethargy. This stuckness often occurs when people assume that accepting what's going on means liking it. It doesn't. You have a right to not like what's happening. But the fact is, it is. No, it's not how you pictured your life turning out. But it's a fact. No, it's not fair. But it's a fact. No, it's not right. But it's a fact. Acceptance is simply about acknowledging the truth of the situation, not approving of it. The difference is crucial.

Interestingly, we may be hardwired to notice when things aren't fair. Research by Friederike Range of the University of Vienna has just discovered that dogs and monkeys both respond to inequity by refusing to participate. If a dog doesn't get rewarded for doing a trick but sees another dog get rewarded for the same trick, it won't do it again. It may even turn away and refuse to look at the person who's been unfair.

For humans, the potential pitfall is falling into a victim mentality. Victims get stuck and refuse to adapt. Without being aware of it, they are making a choice, a choice to stay stuck.

That's what's happened to Karen. Rather than figure out a new way to take care of her kids, she's in danger of blowing up her marriage. What's fascinating about victimhood is, as Hawking points out, it drives people away. That's why a friend of mine says, "You can be the best victim but have the worst future."

I bet you're thinking, I should be so lucky as to have Karen's problem! I'd love to have the chance to stay home with my kids. That's easy to say from the outside. From inside our problems, however, we feel what we feel. I'm not suggesting that you ignore or suppress your feelings. But there is a difference between feeling your emotions and believing them. Because our feelings can be triggered by schemas from the past, they often lie to us. The emotion is real, but the story behind it may not be. That's why our feelings are asking us to relate to them as we would to a child who is going through something difficult. When a child can't get his way, we are nurturing and caring at first, then offer suggestions for making it better and moving on. We can relate to ourselves in the same fashion and avoid the victim trap.

TURN "I CAN'T" INTO "I WON'T"

When people make suggestions as to how you can deal with your situation, do you find yourself stuck in all you *can't* do: "I can't use day care." "I can't renegotiate my divorce settlement." "I can't clean my own bathrooms." "I can't learn a new job." Try this: say instead, "I won't . . ."– "I won't renegotiate my divorce settlement"; "I won't clean my own bathrooms"; "I won't learn a new job." Sounds different, doesn't it? Do you see that it is truly a choice that you're making? What better choice could you make?

Get the 3Cs in Place

All stress is the result of feeling as though you have no
choice about something. As soon as you recognize the
choices inherent in any situation, you regain a sense of being
in control and the feeling of stress will begin to disappear.

—BILL CUMMING

I've been working with Diane, a blind-from-birth woman
in her late forties who's had her share of unasked-for
change. Her husband, who'd been supporting her, died
suddenly. She got a job for the first time in her life, only to
be laid off right when the economy took its 2008 nosedive.
When we first started working together, she told me that
statistically, even in good times, only 20 percent of blind
people are employed.

Psychologists Suzanne Kobasa and Salvatore Maddi are
resiliency experts. In a study of change done on AT&T executives during a reorganization, as well as by analyzing
more than four hundred other studies, they found that
those who thrived better display the 3Cs:

1. Challenge: They saw whatever change befell them as
   a chance to grow and learn, and expressed optimism
   about the future.

2. Control: They believed they could influence their
   lives and the events around them for the better, and
   took actions to make that true. Rather than falling
   into passivity, they looked for the things they could

control and worked on those. They embodied the Serenity Prayer used at AA and other 12-step programs: "Grant me the serenity to accept the things I cannot change, the courage to change the things I can, and the wisdom to know the difference."

3. Commitment: They were passionate about life and saw it as having a deeper meaning than just survival. They stayed connected to people and events even when times got hard.

The 3Cs, Kobasa and Maddi explain in their book, *Resilience at Work*, "amount to the courage and motivation to do the hard but important work of using stressful circumstances to your advantage."

Developing resilience can give you an enormous advantage. According to Al Siebert of the Resiliency Center and author of *The Resiliency Advantage*, research shows that resilient folks perceive change as less threatening, have less of a stress response (fewer stress hormones and lower blood pressure), and respond more creatively. They are more likely to get hired, have more chance of being kept on in a downsizing, are more able to learn new skills when their job is eliminated, are better able to help their families and communities through hard times, and are less likely to get ill under stress. Sign me up!

I asked Diane about her experience with the 3Cs. Diane has a strong willingness to take on a challenge. She'd been living on her own in the house she'd owned with her husband since he died three years before, even though her parents had been begging her to move across the country and in with them. And she was willing to travel around the world. "I see this situation as a chance to learn even more independence," she told me.

"Great," I replied, convinced she'd got the first C nailed. Moving onto control, I asked, "What can you do about your need for income?" "Of course I'd like a job but the odds aren't that good right now. I live in a big house near several universities. I could rent out rooms to graduate students. I think I can make enough to live on if I live simply while I look for work." And that's exactly what she did, as well as reaching out to everyone she knew to let them know she was looking for a job.

When I asked her about her passions, it soon became obvious that she cared deeply about helping young people with disabilities to use new technologies. I encouraged her to look for work in that field. Currently she's reaching out to companies with strong histories of hiring disabled people to see if they have any interest in her running a tech program.

Diane is living proof that connecting more deeply to challenge, control, and commitment is a powerful resource for recovery from a setback. How are you doing on the 3Cs?

Challenge: How could this change be a growth opportunity for you? If you don't know the answer, at least commit to asking the question as you go through your days. It's okay to start with something small or silly—"Now that I don't have a job, I don't have to get dressed up anymore. I can cook more." Or go for the big answers: "I can finally admit I hate being a lawyer."

Control: What can you control here? What actions could you take to be more in control? Even if this change is happening *to* you, there are always things you can control, if only, as Viktor Frankl pointed out in *Man's Search for Meaning,* the meaning you give the event and your response to it.

Commitment: What do you deeply care about? What gives meaning and purpose to your life? What energizes you? How could you get more in touch with those things now?

Think of the 3Cs as ballast. They help you find balance as you ride the waves of change.

WHAT CAN YOU CHANGE THAT IS IN YOUR CONTROL?

In interviewing numerous people for this book, I discovered that when folks found themselves in situations where they had little control, they looked to create change in places they could—getting fit, for instance, or changing appearance, or volunteering at a soup kitchen. Right now, think about one change you can make in your personal, professional, health, relationship, or spiritual life. Pick the one that appeals to you the most. Then go for it. You'll feel better!

Choose Carefully Where You Put Your Attention

There are three kinds of lies: lies, damned lies, and statistics.
—BENJAMIN DISRAELI

"I'd gotten hooked on constantly checking MSNBC and other news sites," Lee said, "until one day I realized it wasn't doing my state of mind any good to look at it over and over. It just scares me into feeling the whole world is falling apart. Now I only look at the news once a day, and it's done wonders for my mood."

As Lee discovered, news focuses on the negative, the extraordinary, and the sensational. This doesn't necessarily serve us well in times of change. For instance, as I write, the headlines are blaring a report that 14.8 percent of the population is underemployed—out of work, given up looking, or working part-time because they can't get a full-time job. That represents millions of people and my heart goes out to those who are dealing with the challenges that number represents. But what if the news reported it the other way—85.2 percent of us are fully employed? How would that change how we're feeling about the state of the country? How about the fact that 30 percent of us own our homes outright and so aren't affected by the mortgage crisis? Bet you never heard that number in the media. I can just see the headline: "One Third of Homeowners Don't Have to Worry."

I was reminded of the importance of keeping perspective when a client of mine told me she'd put her house on the market and bought a condo not contingent on selling her house. Uh-oh, I thought to myself, my mind full of media stories of how home sales have dropped through the floor. What a mistake! She'll end up with two places she can't sell and no way to pay for them both.

A month later, she reported that her house had sold, for only a little less than her asking price, and she'd gotten a much lower mortgage rate on the new place than the old. She's in a better position now for having gone for what she wanted.

The statistics that the news reports tell a story, but not the whole story and not necessarily any individual's story. Yes, home sales are down but that doesn't necessarily mean you can't sell your house. Yes, jobs are hard to find but that doesn't mean you won't be able to find one. Yes, companies

WHAT ANIMAL ARE YOU IMITATING?

Michael Neill, author of *You Can Have What You Want*, suggests that in these times, we are reacting in fear to the media like one or more of the following animals:

- Vole: constantly looking around for predators, spending endless time worrying about fear-inducing scenarios like, "What if the government collapses? What if this downturn lasts for ten years?"

- Ostrich: burying our heads in the sand in denial. "The act itself reveals the fear behind it," he notes. "You don't bury your head . . . unless you are already afraid."

- Fox: acting like a scavenger looking to benefit from the misfortunes of others, fueled by fear. "That just because I have a full stomach today does not mean I'll have a full stomach tomorrow."

Instead he suggests we emulate the lion, who hunts with others "to allow the maximum return for the least effort" and rather than hoarding, shares not only with the pack, but leaves some for other animals.

are downsizing (again!) but that doesn't necessarily mean you will lose your job.

In any given moment, you have the freedom of where you put your attention. You can focus on all the bad news, which most likely creates a sense of hopelessness, or you can focus on what you want to make happen, which creates energy and action. What helps you do the latter? For me, it's limiting my news fix and consciously reminding myself that what I am hearing or reading is a piece of reality, not the whole story.

Avoid Shame by Remembering That Difficulties Can Happen to Anyone

Never build a case against yourself.

—ROBERT ROWBOTTOM

Remember the news frenzy about Ed McMahon, the former sidekick of Johnny Carson, having his house repossessed? He had hurt his neck a while before and couldn't work as a pitchman anymore, so he couldn't make the payments on his mansion and couldn't sell it in the depressed market.

When I read about Ed, I had two responses. My heart went out to him and his wife. And my head thought, yes, it can happen to anyone. No one is immune to a series of unfortunate circumstances coming together and disrupting not only the present but also the anticipated future. In Ed's case it was an injury meeting the down housing market.

Why is it important to remember this? Because when a shocking change happens to us, often one of our first reactions is shame: "It's all my fault." And that doesn't serve us well because shame is an emotion that causes us to want to hide in a hole for a decade or two, rather than take the positive actions we need to in order to get out of the mess.

I'm thinking of a salesman who was laid off six months ago. Joe started working with me recently. He had felt so ashamed over losing his job that he had done nothing to search for a new position. "I don't want to admit I got laid off," he said. I challenged him to give me three plausible reasons why he got laid off that had nothing to do with him. "Well," he replied, "the company has not upgraded the product and so a competitor has a better one. Two, I had never had experience in sales and was actually hired in another position and never received any training in selling. And third, the economy is down in general and so people aren't buying things like this. Hmm. . . . Maybe I'm not such a loser after all."

Here's why shame is so deadly. Once Joe saw that it was not all his fault, he was able to make calls to his network. At the very first one, the other person said, "I wish I'd known sooner. I just hired someone for a job that I would much rather have you for." Joe missed out on a new opportunity because his self-blame created a months-long paralysis.

This is not to say we shouldn't take responsibility for our part in what's happened. Maybe Joe should have insisted he receive training before agreeing to take on the sales job, for instance. But even if we had a big part to play, it's crucial that we remember we were doing the best we could with the information we had at the time. Ed McMahon, for instance, had made a lot of money for decades. So doesn't it make sense that he assumed he would continue to do so?

One of our challenges in change is not to personalize the problem too much. Things happen that we didn't expect and we're often at the mercy of forces, like the housing market, that are definitely beyond our control. When we remember that setbacks happen to the best (and richest) of us, we stay out of shame and are able to get into motion instead. Take the bold step of talking about your situation to others, even if you don't feel like it. "Once you get it out of your head, it's not so ominous," a friend whose business went under confided the other day. "Plus, other people have great ideas that can help."

"FIRED? I'M FIRED UP!"

"I was recently laid off," said Catrina. "At first I fell into a funk. But then I learned that some of the best people in the business have been fired in the past and are back on top. That made me feel confident and defiant. I'm determined to come back stronger than ever. I'll show those folks they made a wrong choice when they let me go!"

Don't Waste Precious Time or Energy on Blame

I do not confer . . . blame: I accept.
—W. SOMERSET MAUGHAM

Recently, I was on the phone listening in to a leadership team meeting of a small business I consult to. Sally, the marketing director, had just said that, due to a mess-up, they would not be able to run the ad they wanted. A good adapter, Sally presented two alternatives—an old ad or a tweaking of wording on the new one that had to be done that day to meet the deadline.

Rather than accept the change and choose the best alternative, the leader kept rehashing the events that led up to the mistake, making accusations and complaining about not getting what he wanted. His business is in deep financial trouble, yet rather than stay focused on the big picture, he took up almost an hour complaining about a tiny problem. He violated one of the main rules of change mastery: forget blame, accept what is, and seek the best solution. Decide afterward if going back over the situation will yield any valuable lessons. If so, it's appropriate to look back. But only if your motivation is to learn for the future. Then it's not blame, but reflection that promotes better performance.

I first learned this principle as a young employee at a weekly newspaper from my mentor Will Glennon. We were understaffed and underfunded; there was always something or someone not working. He was the model of grace as he jumped from fire to fire, providing work around without ever pointing the finger at anyone. I watched and adopted his style. Later, he and I founded Conari Press with no capital whatsoever and we used this capacity to accept and adapt swiftly to build a $6-million company, which at one point was named by *Publishers Weekly* as one of the fastest-growing book publishers in the United States.

Blame is oh so tempting, however. One of the things I've noticed that people do when some difficult change hits is to ask, "Why is this happening? It's got to be someone's fault." We don't want it to be ours, so we find someone else to pin it on: "Oh, it's Mary's fault, not mine, so I can feel a bit better about the fix we're in." It makes us feel more in control to have a why that's not us. But finger-pointing has unintended consequences that are worth understanding.

In *The Unthinkable,* Amanda Ripley points out that people who tend to survive catastrophes such as fire, flood, bombings, kidnappings, etc., accept what's happening more quickly and therefore take action faster than others. Blame is one of those human impulses that creates interference with acceptance. You can't afford the time or mental energy it takes to lay blame, much less to fight with others who want to point the finger at you. You've got more important tasks to attend to. When a tidal wave is about to swamp your boat, it's not the best idea to fight over who's responsible for the fact that you're sitting in a

RESPONSIBILITY, NOT BLAME

Rather than point fingers ("It's all your fault") or fall apart with shame ("It's all my fault"), what we can do is take responsibility for anything we might have done to contribute to the situation. David Burns, in his new book, *Feeling Good Together,* suggests you say something like, "I'll try to identify the errors I've made so I can learn from them and take steps to help resolve the [situation]." Then invite the others involved to do the same.

dinghy rather than a battleship. You just need to pull together and row like mad!

When you find your mind turning to who you can blame for a situation, remember what Confucius said centuries ago: "Things that are done, it is needless to speak about . . . things that are past, it is needless to blame."

Regret Well

To regret deeply is to live afresh.
—HENRY DAVID THOREAU

Tom and Latitia were a young, happily married couple in their late twenties, each busy with their careers and with enjoying their relationship. By the time they got around to starting a family in their midthirties, they encountered fertility problems. Latitia has not been able to get pregnant, despite two years of trying and two rounds of expensive in vitro fertilization attempts. The two of them are kicking themselves now for the choice they made to wait, although there was no way they could have known in advance how things would turn out. Latitia particularly is regretting not trying sooner.

If only I'd . . . Why did I? Why didn't I? What didn't he or she? We all know the painful experience of regret. It feels awful to look back on decisions we made and wish we had made another choice. Hindsight is always 20/20. But we have to live our lives facing forward, without benefit of knowing how it will all turn out, and we have to have mercy for ourselves for not being fortune-tellers. That's why I've always seen regret as a particularly torturous capacity of our minds. What good does it do to beat ourselves up for things we couldn't have known at the time? We did the best we could with what we had.

Still, regret must serve some adaptive purpose or the brain wouldn't have developed the capacity to do it. Psychology professor Neal Roese has written a book on the subject called *If Only*. He says "what if" and "if only" thinking is a biological tool designed for ensuring survival. It exists for us to improve our lives.

"It's a key component of a silently effective brain system by which people comprehend reality, learn from mistakes, move forward, and achieve a bettering of their circumstances," he writes. "Regret is as necessary for healthy living as eating. But like eating, problems arise from both excess and shortfall. It is true that you can suffer too many regrets, making it important to leave the past behind and move on with your life. But so too can you have too few regrets. Neglecting the messages of your own emotions can mean persisting in counterproductive behaviors and missing unique opportunities for growth and renewal."

So how should you handle regret so you get the lessons and don't get stuck in the feeling? Roese offers six strategies:

- *Feel the regret and swiftly move on by using it as a springboard to action.* According to Roese, research shows that successful entrepreneurs are particularly good at this, using mistakes to vault them into improvements of their products, services, and/or organizations.

- *Find more than one reason for what happened.* Yes, you bought two houses, but other people let you, banks were greedy, etc. Coming up with the possible other factors can help you mine the lesson.

- *How could this be worse?* Focusing on how what happened could be worse gives us a burst of positive feeling and helps you keep a wider perspective.

- *Don't spend too much time coming up with all the things you should have done.* It turns out that it's good to think of a few, say three, because it helps you feel in control. But straining to come up with a dozen makes you feel less in control.

- *Tell someone else, either by writing or talking.* "Telling others can improve health, reduce doctor visits, fortify your immune system, and increase life satisfaction," writes Roese. Blogging in particular has been found to be effective because it provides a regular way to reflect, increase self-awareness, and integrate the experience.

- *Keep your eye on the larger picture.* Because the brain has a tendency to narrow its focus under stress, you can end up overfocusing on the problem and your regret. When you keep your eye on the big picture, on "the overall goals for you personally, for your family, or for your organization . . . regret can be brought forward to its highest degree of usefulness."

When Tom and Latitia did this reflection process, they ended up realizing that being parents was more important to them than giving birth to a baby. They decided to adopt a waiting child in the United States and are now the parents of a lively three-year-old.

"I'M KEEPING ON GOING"

Allena Hansen has been viciously attacked by a bear, lost her home in a fire, and broke her back in a horseback riding accident. She now blogs about her life on opensalon .com as a way of healing and staying out of regret and bitterness. In *O* magazine she recently explained how she has managed to get through it all: "When you've lost everything, and I have, eventually you get kind of . . . existential. You simply say, 'This is happening' because all you have is right now. Your choice is either to accept it or let go and die. And I'm keeping on going."

Experience the Comfort of Forgiveness

Life is an adventure in forgiveness.
—NORMAN COUSINS

When the stock market plummeted in 2003 and I lost a third of my savings, I had a very hard time getting over the fact that I didn't see it coming. Some young part of myself still believed I should be all powerful and all knowing. It's a form of magical thinking many of us have developed as a result of growing up in troubled families where we had to take on too much emotional, circumstantial, or even financial responsibility at a young age. We believe we're responsible and "should" be able to foresee the future and solve all problems.

This magical thinking is, of course, a lie, one that gets in the way of accepting our mistakes, learning from them, and moving on. One that has us lashing ourselves over and over with unreasonable, even ludicrous, expectations.

I was thinking about this recently while I was reading an interview in *Gallup Management Journal* with economist Dennis Jacobe, who was asked why people didn't see the recent economic downturn coming. He replied, "There is a principle in behavioral economics called 'overconfidence' that involves believing you will know what will happen in the future to a greater extent than is justified by available information. I think 'overconfidence' dominated people's perceptions during recent years. Nobody believed that housing prices could plummet. Everyone thought that the Fed and the Treasury could contain the financial fallout from the mortgage finance debacle. No one seemed to think you could shatter trust in the modern financial system. All of these almost universally held beliefs turned out to be wrong. . . . Economists were just as guilty of overconfidence as everybody else."

Wow, I thought, if people who do this for a living can make such a big mistake, it makes sense that we who are focused on other things and trained in completely different fields didn't have a clue. All of a sudden, I felt my heart soften toward myself. Greater minds than mine messed up as well, so why should I believe that I should do better than they? I felt the relief of forgiveness as I stopped beating myself up for my now seven-year-old mistake. I saw myself through the eyes of compassion, a perfectly imperfect human being doing the best she could with what she knew at the time.

Of course, often we do have a part to play in what's occurred. Maybe we spent money like a drunken sailor, counting on our houses to continue to go up in value. Or we got complacent in our business, content to do what we've always done rather than pushing ourselves to stay cutting edge. Or we refused to keep up with the times in terms of technology and now we're left behind.

Or perhaps we are where we are due, at least in part, to other people's mistakes and we're angry and resentful— how dare he run up that debt without me even knowing? How could they have run the company into the ground and left me stranded? Why didn't he pull the plug on the stocks sooner? He was in charge, not me!

In the previous chapter, I dealt with mining regrets for the lessons they hold. It's important to do that because it's impossible to truly forgive without learning for the future so you can trust yourself not to repeat your mistake. From what you've learned, you then create a boundary: I won't let that happen again. Only after doing that is it possible to forgive yourself and anyone else.

Much has been written lately about the power of forgiveness to bring us a sense of closure and peace of mind. In some ways, forgiveness is a miraculous mystery. You never know exactly when or how it will arrive, as the story about my lost savings proves. Reading an article seven years after the fact was the thing that allowed me finally to forgive myself for my dot-com bust.

Forcing forgiveness before we are ready only creates a

brittle fake resolution that exists in our heads, not our hearts. I knew I shouldn't beat myself up about the money. But I kept doing it. Spiritual teachers say that, while we can't force forgiveness, we can open our hearts to the desire to forgive and be forgiven through certain practices that help us recognize that we are all imperfect and all deserving of the mercy of forgiveness. In Vispassana Buddhism, for instance, there's a meditation in which you ask for forgiveness and offer forgiveness both to others and to yourself. The practice I include here is by Stephen Levine. Do it when you're ready, knowing it will help create acceptance and closure.

Bring into your heart the image of someone for whom you feel much resentment. Take a moment to feel that person right there in the center of your chest.

And in your heart, say to that person, "For anything you may have done that caused me pain, anything you did either intentionally or unintentionally, through your thoughts, words, or actions, I forgive you."

Slowly allow that person to settle into your heart. No force, just opening to them at your own pace. Say to them, "I forgive you." Gently, gently open to them. If it hurts, let it hurt. Begin to relax the iron grip of your resentment, to let go of that incredible anger. Say to them, "I forgive you." And allow them to be forgiven.

Now bring into your heart the image of someone you wish to ask for forgiveness. Say to them, "For anything I may have done that caused you pain, my thoughts, my actions, my words, I ask for your forgiveness. For all those words that were said out of forgetfulness or fear or confusion, I ask your forgiveness."

Don't allow any resentment you may hold for yourself to block your reception of that forgiveness. Let your heart soften to it. Allow yourself to be forgiven. Open to the possibility of forgiveness. Holding them in your heart, say to them, "For whatever I may have done that caused you pain, I ask your forgiveness."

Now bring an image of yourself into your heart, floating at the center of your chest. Bring yourself into your heart, and using your own first name, say to yourself, "For all that you have done in forgetfulness and fear and confusion, for all the words and thoughts and actions that may have caused pain to anyone, I forgive you."

Open to the possibility of self-forgiveness. Let go of all the bitterness, the hardness, the judgment of yourself.

Make room in your heart for yourself. Say "I forgive you" to you.

Do the Three Blessings

[T]here is always something to be grateful for.

—JON CARROLL

Somehow, *San Francisco Chronicle* columnist Jon Carroll always ends up in my books. I find him so perceptive and witty. For Thanksgiving 2008, he wrote a piece about how practicing gratitude is the antidote to what he called the chasm—the feeling of insecurity and floating unease, caused by the changes underway in our lives and in the world, that is like living on a rickety floor over a cavernous pit.

Try the antidote right now. Take one minute to think of all the things, big or small, you are grateful for in your life. In case you need inspiration, here's my one-minute list: my family and friends, sunshine, novels, the ability to think, the chance to write, the opportunity to work as a thinking partner, hot water, the capacity to learn. Now do your list.

How do you feel? Here's what Carroll says after writing his list: "Can you feel the floor beneath your feet get sturdier? Can you see the holes being patched? For a moment, the bounty of the world overwhelmed you, and you were grateful to be alive at this moment. See? Antidote."

Jon Carroll may not be aware of it, but positive psychology researchers such as Robert Emmons and Martin Seligman have discovered that practicing gratefulness is indeed one of the keys to resilience. People who practice gratitude report higher levels of vitality and less depression and stress during transitions and more easily develop social support in hard times. Researchers have come to understand that when we think grateful thoughts, we activate the part of our brain that releases endorphins, the feel-good hormones, which is what accounts for the positive emotional boost you get.

I can attest to its power. I've spent the last dozen years practicing and writing about thankfulness, and I am still amazed at the uplift I get whenever I think about something I am grateful for, particularly when times are tough for me. It truly is an antidote to feeling like you're falling into the chasm.

I think what is most powerful about gratitude was highlighted many years ago by Br. David Steindl-Rast when he referred to the quality as "great-fullness." When we practice gratitude, we recognize what we have, the bounty of life that is available to us.

That is such an important recognition when we're going through a change not of our choosing. When change is accompanied by loss—of a relationship, a career, life as we knew it—our minds are generally focused on that loss. Practicing gratitude reminds us of all that we still have and all that is still in the world that we can appreciate and enjoy. That's why it's so soothing and healing. It helps us remember our lives in a larger frame than the difficulty we're going through.

I'm not suggesting that you minimize or ignore the difficulty, but that you also include the beauty still available to you. That's why I always tell people gratitude is an "and" experience: Yes, there is challenge . . . and here's what I am thankful for.

I have found thankfulness so very useful in dealing with change that I want to encourage, exhort, and emphasize that you do a daily practice of gratitude. Practice means "to bring something into experience," I just learned. And it's the *experience* of gratefulness that I want you to have as an anchor for turbulent times.

The specific practice I'm going to suggest for you is the Three Blessings created by Martin Seligman. It has been shown by Seligman on his Reflective Happiness website to increase happiness over 90 percent, even for folks who rated themselves as seriously depressed. What you do is every evening, bring to mind three blessings that you are grateful for. Then note your part in making each blessing happen. For instance, (1) I am grateful for the job that came out of the conference call today. My part was to see that there wasn't a conflict between what the client and we wanted, so now he's going to hire us. (2) I'm thankful for sitting down to dinner with my daughter and husband. My part is cooking and creating dinnertime as "our time." (3) I appreciate the feedback I got today on this book. My part was asking for it.

The second part of the practice is as important as the first because it highlights one of the Cs of resilience—control. When you ask yourself what part you had in this blessing, you are reminded that you have control in making good things happen. That's important to remember.

I know what you're thinking. It's what everyone says to me once I describe this exercise: "But what if my blessing is a beautiful sunset or something like that? What's my part in that?" That you noticed. That you are capable of recognizing beauty. That you don't just take for granted the world around you. No matter what you choose to be thankful for, there is a part you play. Your job is to recognize it.

Please do this practice daily, at least for the foreseeable future. It's something that only works when you do it. Do it with your loved ones at the dinner table or before bed. Do it when you're driving home from work. Do it and you'll reap the magic of a great fullness.

Scrolling the website gratefulness.org recently, I noticed that they wrote about gratefulness as "the gentle power that restores courage." We can all use more of that right now.

Cultivate Your Witness Self

[M]editation is a means of cultivating insight through being
mindful of what is arising and passing . . . the aligning and
softening of the heart *to be reconciled with this moment just
as it is* [emphasis added].   —PHILLIP MOFFITT

The other day I got a call from a reporter for a women's magazine wondering if I knew of any new stress-reduction ideas,
"you know, beyond breathing and meditation." It reminded
me of our tendency in this culture to grasp for the novel, and
it even caused me to doubt whether to include this piece in
the book. You would have to have been living under a rock
for the past couple of decades not to know about the benefits of meditation—lower blood pressure and reduced stress,
anger, anxiety, and depression, to name but a few.

But I decided it would be irresponsible of me not to include something that's so effective in accepting the turbulence of change simply because it's been around for
thousands of years. Plus I found something new that I
hope will inspire you to take action if you haven't yet been
convinced to try meditation: new research that shows
you're actually changing your brain structure.

It turns out that "thinking about your thoughts in a
certain way can alter the electrical and chemical activity of
a brain circuit," reports Sharon Begley in *Train Your Mind,
Change Your Brain.* This means that you can permanently
alter how you think through meditation, "strengthening
connections from the thoughtful prefrontal lobes to the
fear- and anxiety-generating amygdala," writes Begley. And

a recent study in the *Proceedings of the National Academy of Sciences* found that you can get meditation's fabulous effects in as little as three minutes a day! "The brain responds to repetition with more gusto than duration," says Daniel Siegel, associate clinical professor of psychiatry at UCLA. So you don't have the excuse that you don't have time.

The study also found that meditation is more effective than the popular stress-reduction technique of guided relaxation in which you consciously relax one part of your body after another. Here's my speculation as to why, which says something about why meditation is such a crucial tool in AdaptAbility. Unlike guided relaxation, meditation strengthens the "witness self"—the part of our minds that is aware of our thoughts and feelings.

The more we strengthen that part, the more we're not just living on automatic pilot, at the mercy of our conditioned responses or feelings, but are able to be more deliberate in how we respond. We understand that thoughts are not facts and that we can observe our fearful, sad, or angry thoughts come and go rather than being at their mercy. Dawna calls it holding the kite string to your mind so you can direct where it goes rather than letting it go wherever it's blown.

This is a crucial capacity during change because it both allows you to register what you are feeling *and* ask yourself, "What is the most skillful way to respond to circumstances right now?" With a strong witness self, we're no longer at the whim of our unconscious behavior, but are behind the wheel of our destiny, more able to adapt and adjust with ease.

If I've inspired you to give it a try, here's a very basic form of mindfulness meditation:

• Find a quiet place to sit in a chair or on the floor, with your eyes open or closed, whichever is most comfortable to you. Set a timer for the amount of time you plan to sit.

• Become aware of your breathing, focusing on the sensation of air moving in and out of your body as you breathe.

• When thoughts come up in your mind, whether worrying, planning, or wishing, don't try to ignore or suppress them. Simply note them and return your awareness to your breath without judging yourself, no matter how many times you do it.

• When the timer goes off, get up gradually.

LOVING KINDNESS MEDITATION

This practice comes from the Vipassana Buddhist tradition. It is an offering of kind wishes to yourself and others. It can be done anywhere, anytime. I started doing it when I was going through a difficult time in my publishing company and felt helpless. I'd wake up in the night worrying. This gave me something else to do. It operates on the principle that the energy of well-wishing helps bring the good result into being. And even if that is not true, it creates happiness as you offer kindness and compassion to yourself, those you know, and all those you don't. Plus research by Harvard psychology professor Richard Davidson has found that such compassion meditation can reduce activity in your amygdala. Sit or lie down quietly.

The point is to find four or five phrases that represent what you most wish for yourself and others. Think to yourself, "What do I wish most for myself and for those I love?"

Here are mine:

[You begin with yourself]

May I be peaceful,

May I be happy,

May I be safe and protected,

May I be free from suffering,

May I be filled with loving kindness.

[Then bring someone close to you to mind and say the same to him or her]:

May ____ be peaceful,

May ____ be happy,

May ____ be safe and protected,

May ____ be free from suffering,

May ____ be filled with loving kindness.

[Keep on going until you have included everyone you want to, moving from those close to you and ending with]:

May all beings be peaceful,

May all beings be happy,

May all beings be safe and protected,

May all beings be free from suffering,

May all beings be filled with loving kindness.

Stay Open to Miracles

You are always in a universe of choices. Any moment of your
life can go in any direction you choose. . . . Learn to choose.

—LUIS ALBERTO URREA

I've known Cindy my whole life. She's now forty-eight.
Adopted at birth by an alcoholic mother and a workaholic
father, she pretty much raised herself. She got to school in
the morning, made dinner in the evenings, figured out her
homework by herself. Her mother was even too drunk to
visit her in the hospital when she was in a serious car accident when in her twenties.

She has had her share of anger and grief about her family situation. But somehow, she always chose to stay connected to her parents. She called every Sunday, drove three
hours each way with her husband and kids to visit regularly. It got easier when her mother sobered up in the early
nineties, but there was still hurt as her mother never apol-
ogized for her behavior. Her dad died a few years ago, and
last year her mother, now elderly, decided to move five
minutes away from her. Cindy packed up her house and
helped her buy a new place. She takes her out to dinner,
shopping, to doctor appointments. When we speak, I
often marvel that she is so willing to care for someone who
never cared for her. "She's the only mother I have," Cindy
responded.

Then Cindy broke her ankle very badly and developed
a deep vein thrombosis that could have killed her. It was a

wave of change from left field. She couldn't work for months and needed help doing even the basics of daily living. "You'll never believe what happened," she told me one day. "My mother saved me. She cooked dinners, picked up and dropped off the kids at school. She even cleaned my house! She was finally there for me in a way that she never could be before. On Mother's Day, I thanked her and she responded she was glad that she'd been given a second chance to be my mother. We both cried tears of happiness."

I thought about the hundreds of hours I had been witness to Cindy's pain. Both of us had written off her mother as incapable of caring or apologizing. Neither of us could ever have anticipated this healing moment.

I thought of Cindy recently when I got a letter from a reader of my book *The Power of Patience*. The writer detailed some horrible things he'd gone through, which resulted in his losing his license to practice medicine, and how some people had taken a chance on him, so that he was now back at work, grateful for the second chance.

Until the exact second we die, the possibility for miracles in our lives exists. We can't force the miracle, we can't demand it of ourselves or others, we can't predict how or when it might occur. But we can, like Cindy, keep ourselves available to its possibility by not closing the little door to our hearts.

This openness is different from holding on to illusions that keep us stuck—wishing the guy would walk back in the door when he hasn't returned our six hundred phone calls, or that a magic fairy will keep our house from being repossessed. We've got to face reality. As Rabbi Harold Kushner wrote, "It's okay to pray for a miracle as long as you're also working to deal with your problem."

Whenever we suffer a setback from some unwanted change, the miracle of a second chance is possible, particularly when we let go of our ideas of what, how, and when it "should" be and make ourselves available to whatever wonders might occur. San Francisco Bay Area newspapers were filled a while ago with a story about a couple in their late forties whose two children were killed by a drunk driver a few years ago and have just given birth to a baby girl. The egg donor was the mother's niece. Not only that, but when the niece came to donate, she met the young man next door, and they got married and are expecting a baby of their own.

When you're going through a painful change, it may be hard to imagine a future moment when a second chance blossoms in front of you. I know, for instance, when I was suffering from a back injury in my twenties and thirties, that I could not envision being a pain-free fifty-five year old. Or when I was dumped and alone at age forty that I would ever have a wonderful husband and daughter. I know that the younger Cindy would not have believed in the Mother's Day she just had with her mother.

So, right now, know that I'm keeping the faith for you. The faith that there's a second chance in your future. And I hope that reading other people's miracles will help you, even a little bit, through this hard place.

Find the Gift in the Change

No bad can befall us that does not bring us some good.

—LUIS ALBERTO URREA

Bill Harris had a very small audio recording business and was struggling to make ends meet when he was sued for a million dollars for copyright infringement. His lawyers told him that it could cost up to $150,000 or more to defend his case. Tossing and turning at night, he remembered reading that there are always benefits hidden in any challenging change. At first he couldn't think of any, but he kept asking himself, "What could be the benefit be of this?"

"In asking this question," he says in *The Resiliency Advantage* by Al Siebert, "I began to dream." If his company Centerpointe was worth $150,000 to defend, he reasoned, he'd have the kind of company that would be advertising in national magazines and have lots of employees and be making millions of dollars. He'd be a successful speaker at conferences and a published author.

Instead of giving up, he started taking the actions, like advertising, he had dreamed up, which led to his growing the company into a hugely successful one (and settling the lawsuit for only $7,000 in legal fees, by the way). "The 'disaster' turned out to be a benefit in disguise. Without it, Centerpointe would probably have limped along for another year or so and then quietly gone to small-business heaven. All of this happened because I looked for the potential benefits in what seemed to be a major disaster, then took action to make those potential benefits a reality."

One of the things I've noticed as I've witnessed folks go through all kinds of changes—from cancer and divorce to job losses, bankruptcies, suicide of a loved one, and even imprisonment—is that the people who grow through the unwanted change have the ability to see the gift in the wound, to seek—and find—a benefit to what's happened to them.

What's the gift in this change for you? At the beginning, when your emotions may be raw, this question may seem downright insulting. But there's always a gift to be found in what happens to us, and it helps create emotional resolution to look for what that might be. Even torture victims who've been granted asylum in the United States are being trained in specialized support groups to look at what positive qualities they cultivated as a way to heal.

You shouldn't look for the gift on the day you get the bad news. But please do so at some point in the process. Here are some questions to get you going:

- If anything could be right about this change for me, what could it be?

- How can I take this situation and turn it to my advantage?

- What opportunities has this created that I could take advantage of? This last is a classic entrepreneurial question because successful businesses can always be created from difficult situations.

Whatever answers you discover are a portal to acceptance—and a better tomorrow.

STEP 2: EXPAND YOUR OPTIONS

Not knowing when the dawn will come, I open every door.

—HELEN KELLER

Remember the example I gave in the introduction about how easily we adapt to small changes? If a friend canceled your dinner plans, your first step would be to say, "Okay, that's out." Then you'd think about the remaining options—stay home, call up someone else, eat out alone. Which you choose is not likely to make a huge difference in the long run.

However, when a change is complex or big, how you think about your available options is crucial because it's likely that you actually need to think and/or behave differently than before to come up with the most effective response. As Einstein reminded us, "The significant problems we have cannot be solved at the same level of thinking with which we created them." That's what this part of the process of AdaptAbility is all about. You want to make sure you've considered all the possibilities and look at the situation from as wide a perspective as possible. That way you'll increase the possibility of success once you move into action.

You'll discover why change may exhilarate you while it frightens a loved one or vice versa, which has a lot to do with your persistent ways of thinking. You'll also learn how to connect more deeply to your passions, talents, values, and resources, which are the raw materials you take with you into any situation. The more you know what those enduring elements are, the more you can create a future of success and fulfillment. For one of the upsides when change hits us is that we're given a golden opportunity to revisit our lives and ask where we want to be and what we want to be doing now.

What Helps You Expand Your Thinking?

A "creative" is anyone who creates. Anything. . . . Everyone on the planet is creative.   —STEFAN MUMAW and WENDY LEE OLDFIELD

Imagine you're a fly on the wall of my house as I work. What would you see? Some days, I'm on the phone all day talking to clients. On those days, I have a headset on and wander from room to room. Other days, when I'm writing, I alternate between typing at my computer and jumping up to go into my backyard. Am I hyperactive? Do I have ADD? Actually, it is very easy for me to sit in one spot unmoving for hours. So why all the jumping around? Because I've discovered that movement helps me be at my most creative, innovative, and imaginative, and I want to access that part of myself when I'm working.

When adapting to change, we need to come up with thoughts and solutions that are different from ones we've used in the past. Otherwise we will just be responding in habitual ways that may not serve us now. That's why, in the expanding phase of AdaptAbility, we first need to know how to access our most creative thinking.

We tend to think about creativity in the context of being an artist or musician. However, I prefer the definition that resiliency expert Frederic Flach uses. Creativity is "a response to a situation that calls for a novel but adaptive solution, one that serves to accomplish a goal." We can all be creative—under the right circumstances.

The crucial question is not, am I creative, but what conditions allow me to be at my most creative in my thinking? For each of us, there is a different answer. I wander, but Angie needs to listen to music without any words and then talk to someone who says nothing but just receives what she has to say. Louis needs to scribble on a white board or doodle on paper.

You may already know what works for you. If so, great. Go for it. If not, one way to figure out your best way is to think about when you have your best ideas. What were you doing? For Will, it's when he's on a golf course. For Grace, it's when she's journaling. For Patrick, it's when he talks to his wife. Your formula may be easy to see once you pay attention.

If you're not sure, do an experiment. I'm going to give you three creativity exercises I've adapted from *Caffeine for the Creative Brain* by Stan Mumaw and Wendy Lee Oldfield (Your task is not just to come up with answers, but also to observe what you did to get your creative thinking flowing): (1) In the era of cell phones, phone booths are pretty irrelevant. Come up with ten alternative uses for a phone booth, with or without phones, your choice. (2) Without using the word *exit*, develop an alternative to an exit sign in a building that indicates the way out. (3) Imagine that a stick is the hottest kids' toy. What would they do with it? What tricks and games could they play?

A pattern should emerge of what helps you generate ideas and possibilities. (This only works if you actually do the exercises!) Note it and use it as you go through this step. You want to bring your most innovative thinking to bear here.

For more help, go to PTP's website: www.ptp-partners .com. Our work is based on understanding the differences between people's minds and can help you understand yours and use it most effectively. Look at the tools for discovering and using your Mind Pattern, which is what we call your brain's particular sequence of organizing, deciding, and creating. The more you know how to use the instrument that is your mind, the more productive and successful you'll be overall. And the more you will be able to think creatively whenever you need to.

CREATE AN AVATAR

Online worlds like Second Life invite you to create an alter ego with any characteristics you want. Why not take advantage of the brain's capacity to do that in this life, where it really matters? If you are having trouble accessing your own creativity or have a belief that you're not creative which is standing in your way, how about creating an avatar who is highly innovative and imaginative? He has already faced this exact situation and found some great solutions. Give him a name and characteristics. When you're stuck, call on him to help. Think, "What would [your avatar's name here] suggest doing right now?"

How Does Your Self-Concept Need to Change?

There is no meaning to life except the meaning man gives to
his life by the unfolding of his powers.   —ERICH FROMM

Mike has been an agent for TV scriptwriters for twenty
years. "I don't handle actors," he proclaims, "too much
trouble." Here's the problem: during the recent writers'
strike, he didn't make a penny for nine months. And since
then, business for scriptwriters has been very limited. The
TV industry isn't making as much money as it used to and
is reluctant to spend money on scripts when it can do
much cheaper reality shows. But Mike is unwilling to
change with the times: "I only handle writers," he insists.
To put it mildly, he has a problem with adapting.

Each of us as we grow up forms an idea of ourselves. By
the time we're adults, it's pretty fixed. Psychologists call it a
self-concept. You can quickly figure out yours by filling in
the sentence "I'm a person who . . ." Here's mine: "I'm a
person who's smart, practical, and dependable, who worries
a lot, who reads, writes, and talks for a living, who needs a
lot of sleep, who's highly analytic and relational but not very
creative. . . ." I could go on, but you get the idea.

Our self-concept gives us security. We know what we
can count on in ourselves. But, as we saw with Mike, a self-
concept also creates limitations in our thinking and behavior that can be a problem when we're faced with a situation
in which we need to adapt. Without our knowing it, our
self-concept limits our options because it puts walls around
who we think we are and what we can or will do.

I was thinking of this recently when I worked with a person for the first time. I was going on and on about how I'm not innovative, and he looked at me and said, "That's not my experience of you. You've already come up with several great ideas I never thought of." Hmm, I thought, he's onto something. In fact, I have come up with several innovative book ideas that sold really well. Maybe I need to revise my self-concept. I may not be the most innovative thinker on the planet, but that doesn't mean I don't ever have new ideas.

What's your self-concept? Pick up a pen and write down your answers to the sentence "I am a person who . . ." Keep going until it becomes an effort. Then look at the qualities, habits, and behaviors you've written down. They're all true, I'm sure. But what happens if the change you're facing challenges some or all of them? What if you're being asked to expand your notion of who you are in order to meet the realities of life as it is now, not how it used to be? Change always asks us to expand our idea of ourselves, to tap powers we never knew we had, to cultivate new qualities, habits, and ways of being. We can't do that with a rigid self-concept.

For me, for instance, what if opportunities to make a living writing and coaching dry up, as they could very well do? What does that do for my self-concept as a writer and thinking partner? If I hold that idea of myself too tightly, I can get stuck if I have to look for another line of work.

Look at your self-concept again. How does it need to be revised to meet the challenges of change? Think for a moment about the hurdles you've faced so far in your life. What experiences have you grown from that aren't included in your self-concept? What qualities have others seen in you that aren't represented?

When I think about those questions for myself, here are my additions to my self-concept: I'm someone who is . . . a survivor, a learner, more creative than I give myself credit for, a person who knows how to ask for help. Unlike my original one, this expanded self-concept can really help me if I need to change careers.

What about you? You have powers beyond your idea of yourself. Now's the time to bring them to awareness.

ROOT OUT OLD NEGATIVE ASSUMPTIONS

"For years, people told me that I wasn't a people person," said Sonia. "And I just accepted it without thinking. But when I went through a process of looking at what I really love to do, I came to see that mentoring is not just something I love but I'm really good at!" What assumptions are you making about yourself because of limiting comments from others? Don't face change carrying other people's assumptions of you. Take a moment to think about the damning remarks you've been told that you accept as truth—"You have no willpower," "You'll never make anything of yourself," "You're not the mother type"—and find three examples from your life that disprove them. Then when you catch yourself thinking that poisonous thought, bring an example that disproves it to mind and say to yourself, "That's their story about me, not my story about myself."

Seek Information Outside Your Box

If the only tool you have is a hammer, you tend to see every
problem as a nail.   —ABRAHAM MASLOW

I was working with a number of executives in a company
that was going public and growing by acquisitions. Both
are dramatic changes and the company was doing them simultaneously. The whole organization was under tremendous strain, and so were the folks I was talking to.

One day, I said to one, "Other companies have gone
through similar changes. Who do you know that you could
talk to about this who could give you some advice?" She
said she didn't know anyone to ask. I asked my other
clients the same question. Not one of them knew anyone
they could speak to. When I commented on this to one of
them she replied, "Yes, it's part of our company culture not
to create outside networks but to rely on ourselves." Interestingly, shortly thereafter, the CEO of this company was
fired by the board precisely because of his unwillingness to
seek outside advice.

Rightly so, I'd say. For they made one of the crucial
mistakes you can during change—to assume that what you
already know and are doing are the right things to do
under new circumstances. It's a natural assumption, particularly when you've met with success in the past. In a certain way, this CEO and his executives were victims of their
own success. They didn't think they needed to learn something new to cope with the situation they were in.

It made me think of a fish experiment. Baby fish were put in a little tank inside a larger fish tank. They grew up and swam around in the small tank and eventually the scientists took away the walls of the smaller tank. Guess what? The fish continued to swim in the same small configuration, despite being in the larger tank. Like those fish, we put limits around our thinking because we're used to swimming around in a certain way that's worked for us so far. Marshall Goldsmith talks about this danger in his book whose title says it all: *What Got You Here Won't Get You There.* I'd modify that message slightly to "what got you here doesn't always get you there and the trick is to know when it won't."

One way to avoid that pitfall is to be sure to seek information outside your own box when change is upon you. Find mentors who've done what you're about to. They've been through it and can offer valuable information regarding the journey you're about to embark on. Also seek out what some are calling reverse mentors, meaning young people who, because they haven't worked for decades inside organizations, have totally fresh ways of approaching life and work. Remember, it was the oldest people who got into trouble during Hurricane Katrina because they allowed their past experience to guide them. When you're in the unknown, sometimes experience gets in the way. If you get both perspectives, you're getting the best of both worlds.

The worst thing you can do right now is isolate, despite the urge to hunker down and try even harder to do what you're doing. Yes, it takes more energy to go out there and get outside input, but it's necessary. Organizational consultant Meg Wheatley talks about the fact that the more information-rich your environment, the more intelligent your choices.

So get out there and swim outside your own tank. Right now, brainstorm who you can speak to, to get an outside perspective. And each time you talk to someone, finish with the question, "Who else do you think I should speak with about this?"

Hedge Your Bets

We must learn to explore all the options and possibilities that confront us in a complex and rapidly changing world.

—J. WILLIAM FULBRIGHT

Did you ever learn that proverb "Don't put all your eggs in one basket?" I've been thinking a lot about it recently, after hearing about a friend of a friend who works for Citigroup. She'd gotten compensated partly in company stock, which she just let sit there rather than diversifying her portfolio; when the stock tanked, so did her life savings. Contrast that with my friend Jackson who, every time he got company stock, sold it and bought a variety of investments.

I've always believed in spreading risk around as much as possible. I learned this accidentally. When my then partner and I were building a house, we couldn't afford to carry the full mortgage. So we created a separate kitchen on the downstairs level and rented out a third of our house. Later, when we broke up, I specifically looked for a house that had a rental attached. It gave me great comfort to know that if my income was drastically reduced, I had a money stream. However, not quite getting the lesson, I later bought a house without a rental and ended up having to sell it precisely because I couldn't afford it when my income took a downturn. You can bet that the house I now own has a rental!

This doesn't just apply to houses. Since I left publishing, I've built a career with three aspects—writing, working with clients, and ghostwriting for other people. Over the years, when one aspect has dipped, another has risen so the three taken together have seen me through. And I try to continually expand my client base so that when one disappears, I still have work.

The underlying principle here is that greater stability is found when you spread the risk by having more than one option. That's always true, but particularly in times of great turbulence when you don't know what the future is going to bring. It's called hedging your bets.

In this society, we tend to glorify those who take a huge risk by investing all they have to make their one dream come true. The problem is that we never hear about those for whom such all-or-nothing behavior didn't work. A friend of mine just got funding for his company after years of sweat equity and depleting his own savings. He was on the verge of losing his house when venture capitalists came to the rescue. I took him to lunch to celebrate and was praising him for his single-minded dedication and willingness to risk it all. He looked at me and said, "Yes, but I would never recommend it to anyone because it so easily could have gone the other way and I would have nothing right now. If I had it to do over, I'm not sure I would do it."

Having a plan B or something to fall back on is a smart strategy. I think of two acquaintances, both of whom run small businesses. One is a manufacturer—she reports her U.S. business has really dried up, but the overseas one is carrying the company. Good thing she had the foresight to develop both. The other runs a structural engineering company. Her residential business has completely disappeared, but a year ago, seeing that relying only on that was risky, she'd expanded into commercial real estate and is hanging in there.

What about the situation you're in? How can you hedge your bets? The rest of this section will give you strategies for expanding your thinking. Right now, I'd like you just to begin to explore in your own mind what expanding your options would mean for you: Creating a greater network of contacts inside and outside your orga-

GIVE UP FOR A WHILE

I'm sure you've noticed that when you try to solve a problem and get stuck, if you get up and do something else, particularly something mindless like take a shower or wash the floor, the answer suddenly pops into your head. The reason is that when you're "trying," your brain is activating certain parts and blocking others so you can focus. When you give up, the blocking turns off and your brain is in touch with more of its resources. So when you get stuck, give up and clean up those files or rearrange the silverware drawer. It will help you expand your thinking.

nization? Taking in a boarder? Getting training in another field? Teaming up with someone else?

Hedging your bets gives you a valuable sense of security. A client of mine just went to a going-away party for a colleague and got offered a job by a competitor. He's feeling better now about his position with his company because he's got more than one option.

Kill Your Little Darlings

I think all great innovations are built on rejections.

—LOUISE NEVELSON

When I was an editor, I always loved the quote attributed to William Faulkner that writers needed to "kill their little darlings." It's a message about how, in order for inspiration to enter, we need to let go of the ideas we're so in love with in order to make room for something better. It's a willingness that everyone needs to succeed these days.

I was reminded of this when I read a recent cover story in *Fortune* on why J.P. Morgan is doing better in the financial markets meltdown than other investment banks. The article focuses on CEO Jamie Dimon's leadership style and points out that Dimon is known not only for holding strong opinions but also for truly listening to others and letting go of his passionate position when someone on his team presents a compelling argument to do so. His leadership meetings are like "Italian family dinners," with everyone throwing out their opinions vociferously. Said Bill Daley, the head of corporate responsibility and a former secretary of commerce, "People were challenging Jamie, debating him, telling him he was wrong. It was nothing like I'd seen in a Bill Clinton cabinet meeting, or anything I'd ever seen in business."

What the article implies is that one of the keys to J.P. Morgan's success is that Dimon has a mind that is willing to be influenced, to let go of treasured beliefs. He is willing to kill his little darlings.

This is a huge competitive advantage during times of change. The willingness to be influenced makes us open to new information when it arrives rather than stay loyal to our own surety or status as "the one in charge." Contrast that with a CEO I know who is leading his organization into bankruptcy. He refuses to listen to the people he hired to advise him because he's so attached to the belief that he knows best. The people around him have given up trying and are quietly looking for other jobs.

How does this apply to you? We all have beliefs we hold on to. Under stress, we tend to hold tighter, which is precisely the opposite of what we should be doing. When things around us are changing, rather than clutching our opinions like a security blanket, we need to hold them up to the light and examine them closely and critically. That means having a willingness to admit, even if only to yourself, that you don't have all the answers. Therefore, you invite challenges and seek out contrary opinions: "Tell me where my thinking is wrong here." "What am I missing?" "What else should we be considering?"

There's a fabulous movie called *Thirteen Days,* about the Cuban missile crisis. In it, you see JFK, who had previously accepted unquestioningly what the generals told him about the Bay of Pigs operation, leading to a fiasco, now asking all kinds of "dumb" questions and refusing to accept the experts' assumptions. Many historians believe that it was his refusal to heed his generals that averted a nuclear war. He insisted that his advisors find another way.

Like JFK, when we're entering unknown territory, as much as possible we should seek out people and situations that challenge our assumptions. And be willing to ask dumb questions and give up on our most cherished ideas when a better one comes along. As the Chinese proverb says, "To be uncertain is to be uncomfortable, but to be certain is ridiculous." Important words for our times.

Tap into Your Inner Resources

Success is to be measured not so much by the position that one has reached in life as by the obstacles which he has over-come.   —BOOKER T. WASHINGTON

Dave is one of us who got caught up in the real estate boom and bought two houses to flip. Now they are not worth the mortgages and he can't get rid of them. Frozen in fear, he came to me. I asked him to name the hardships he'd faced in the past. He came up with getting laid off four times in his career, going through a divorce, and dealing with the drug addiction of his teenage son. Then I asked him to think about the inner qualities of mind and heart that he had cultivated as a result of each of these challenges.

"Well," he responded, "getting laid off and then finding

other jobs really helped me to become more proactive. I also had to create greater self-confidence and a sense of my own value, despite other people's opinion of me. Getting divorced allowed me to understand that I could go through difficult feelings and survive, and that I can reach out for help, something that was very hard for me to do before that. Dealing with my son cultivated an ability to block out empathy when necessary because to help him I had to learn to say no. And to understand that life is all about learning and growing." "Great," I replied, "now how would you use those resources in the situation you're in now?"

Like all of us, Dave is doing his best to cope with the knocks that change dishes out. Part of being human means we can't go through life without life going through us, and as it does, it tends to rip, bend, and fold. The good news is that every time we go through something challenging, we develop strengths and awareness we didn't have before. We grow wiser, more resilient in very specific ways. These are strengths we can call upon the next time a wave knocks us down.

To my mind, that's one of the beauties of life, because it makes meaning of our suffering. We're not just tossed about mindlessly in the sea of change. We learn and grow so it's easier the next time we find ourselves in the water. Studies of police and firefighters have found, for instance, that they often fare well after a life-and-death emergency because they recognize that they saved themselves once and therefore can do it again. Someone once told me that fearlessness is the confidence that you will be able to gather the inner resources necessary to deal with whatever comes your way. That's why it's so important to know what those are.

Unfortunately, many of us don't take the opportunity to reflect on what we've learned from our past difficulties, making our inner resources less available for the change we're going through. It's like having a bank account you never tap into, even when you need it, because you're not aware of its existence. When you live like this, each challenge is its own scary monster that you feel powerless to slay.

I want you to understand the qualities you've cultivated so you can use all the resources available to you to think through your response to the change you face. We're going to talk about outer resources in the next chapter. Now we're concentrating on your inner ones.

I'm going to ask you to do the same exercise I gave Dave. Think of the major challenges in your life so far. Reflect on the qualities and understanding you gained as a result of going through them. Then apply what you've learned to the current situation.

Here's what Dave said when he thought about his real estate crisis through the lens of what he'd cultivated in himself: "It helps me to remember that I've survived other challenges before. I know I can live through this, too. And like when I was looking for work, I need to be proactive in finding out what programs the government and banks might have, rather than sitting around worrying. I'm going to search out all the available help."

What if you've never faced a hardship before? Life has been kind to you and you've never weathered a storm. You still have had successes—finishing school, starting a family, getting a job. Name your successes to yourself and think about the qualities of heart, mind, and spirit you used to create those accomplishments. Those are your inner resources. For instance, Jeffrey is a young man who is faced with a debilitating disease. He has a PhD in biology. When I asked him to mine his successes for inner resources he said, "Well, I am great at doing research, so I can use that to cope with my illness. Plus I have a lot of drive and determination to succeed that I used to climb the ladder of science. I can use that now to conquer this disease!"

Connecting to your inner resources will help you calm down and move into action. You've handled hard things or made things happen before. You can do this, too!

ASK YOUR FUTURE SELF FOR HELP

If you're stuck on what to do, imagine it's a year from now and you've dealt with the situation in such a way that you are really satisfied. Your future self has lived through this moment, and is wiser for it. That future self comes back to this moment to tell you something you need to know to get from here to there. What does the future self say?

What Other Resources Are Available?

All truths are easy to understand once they are discovered; the point is to discover them.   —GALILEO

Catherine went through a painful divorce that left her in bad financial shape with two young children to support and no job. Initially she felt overwhelmed and scared. By the time she wrote to me, she'd done a pretty good job of accepting the situation and she was trying to figure out what to do. First I helped her become more aware of her inner qualities that could help her through. "Persistence, a kind of toughness that says I won't let this bring me down, and an ability to be resourceful" were the ones she noted.

Then I suggested that she become more aware of her outer resources. These are things that you can draw on in your environment, such as time, money, and other people. "Well, my ex is paying child support and alimony that will last for two years. So that's money I can use to buy myself some time. Plus, my dad is willing to help me if he can. And I have a friend who keeps inviting me to work as a waitress in his diner."

Armed with those resources, Catherine created a plan. She would get a degree in accounting while working part-time for her friend so that by the time she lost the alimony payment, she'd have a better chance at a well-paying job. Her dad would babysit so she could attend night classes and he even offered to pay for the training itself.

Just like inner resources, we all have outer resources, things and people outside of ourselves that we can call on when and if we need to. Now is the time to make those visible to yourself. Right now, make a list of your outer resources. Don't dismiss anything because of a perceived obstacle—the brother you haven't spoken to in years; the 401k that supposedly can't be touched. You may be surprised to discover there is no obstacle after all. For instance, I just read of companies that are helping entrepreneurs get cash out of their 401ks without penalty to use in their businesses.

List everything and everyone that could be useful: the land you could turn into a vegetable garden, the fancy car you might be able to sell, the equity in a house you've had for a long time, the friend who may be able to give you a loan. The more you are aware of what you have to work with, the better you will feel—and the more options you will have when it's time to make a plan.

"IT BROUGHT US TOGETHER AGAIN"

"It's been a rough year," said Helen. "My furniture import business failed and my boyfriend of three years dumped me. I had been estranged from my family for years because they hadn't wanted me to go off on my own and start a business. But they were my best resources for helping me get back on my feet. So I swallowed my pride and contacted them. My sisters did do a bit of the 'We told you sos,' but overall they welcomed me back with open arms and helped me get set up in a studio apartment and allowed me to join the family business again. I'm still healing from the pain of what's happened, but am grateful that it brought us back together again."

Be Like the Native Americans

I am where I am because I believe in all possibilities.
—WHOOPI GOLDBERG

I was on the phone with Sheila. We'd been working together to help her become the director of a nonprofit she'd been working at for ten years. She'd been aiming for the directorship for years and thought she had it in the bag. Now the situation had changed. The board had rearranged personnel so the path that Sheila had imagined to the top had been cut off. She was in despair, ready to walk out the door, pitching a fit as she departed. "I knew I couldn't get what I wanted," she cried. "I never do. I'm devastated."

"Of course you are," I replied. "This is a setback. You had a specific idea in mind and now it's gone. When you see only one option, it's like being a bunny in a hole and a fox is poking its nose into your only escape route. Your emotional brain senses danger and you go into fight or flight. What's needed is for you to build a number of other doors so your emotional brain calms down and your thinking brain takes over. I want you to think of seven possible ways to respond to this situation."

"Why seven?" she asked.

"Because the Native Americans say that if you can't think of seven options, your thinking is incomplete. I'm not sure there's something magical about the number except that it allows you to generate a lot of possibilities. It's okay if they aren't all realistic. This is a brainstorm."

"Okay. One, I could quit. Two, I could accept that I will never be boss. Three, I could stay resentfully in the position I am in now. Four, I could shoot the new head of the board of directors who is standing in my way. Five, I could complain behind her back to everyone in the company so they hate her, too. Six, I could befriend her and help her so she sees I am invaluable; then later, when she's an ally I can let her know my desire to head the organization. Seven, I could go to the board and demand they pick between us right now."

"What do you really want and which of these would be most likely to get you what you want?" I asked.

"I really love this organization and would love to head it. I'm not sure I could find another situation that is as good for me. The best idea would be to befriend the woman."

So that's exactly what she did. And now, a year later, Sheila is indeed running the company. She didn't get the title she'd imagined for herself, but in all other ways, including salary, she's gotten her heart's desire.

When change creates obstacles that get in the way of what we want, it's a natural human tendency to fall into self-pity, anger, or resentment. It comes from feeling like the trapped rabbit. But by expanding our thinking, we can find a way out.

I've done this with hundreds of people, and it really works—as long as we are willing to let go of it being precisely the way we first imagined. So many times we get hung up on the "how" and lose sight of the "what." That's why I asked Sheila what she really wanted. The more you know that, the more you are willing to find alternative routes, keeping in mind your desired destination. Sheila didn't get the big title, and she and I had to work through that, too. She realized that the job was more important to her than what it was called, so she could let that go. But she would never have gotten the job offer at all if she hadn't expanded her thinking when she felt trapped.

Recently a friend of mine, Denise, who lives in New York City, went through a divorce and was trying to figure out how to reduce her monthly expenses. She realized when all was said and done, her car cost her $900 a month.

"But I can't live without a car," she wailed to a friend. Her friend helped her see that she had other options. "Today," she proudly proclaimed to me recently, "I am an expert at renting cars. I know how to get the best deals and who will deliver a car right to your office."

There is always more than one way to deal with your situation, even when it's not of your choosing and you'd rather have different options. If you can't do it easily yourself, do this brainstorm with a friend. When we look at

---

WHAT'S THE NEXT BEST OPTION?

If you're stuck in your thinking and can't come up with seven options because you're fixated on what you want that you can't have, ask yourself, "What's the next best option?" That's what Rachel did. Every summer she and her family rented a cabana at a beach club, had done so for ten years. Her husband is a hedge fund manager whose fund collapsed, and they needed to cut out all unnecessary expenses until he could get back on his feet. Rachel was really upset about the beach club—she felt like she was taking something important away from her kids. We talked about the second best option, which was to rent a locker at the same club rather than a full cabana (about a third of the price) and set up camp at a friend's cabana during the days as needed. Will it be ideal? No. But it will enable her to keep what's important to her, which is a place for her city children to go on summer weekends. What's your version of the next best option?

multiple possibilities, we increase our sense of freedom and therefore increase the likelihood of a satisfying result. Otherwise, we tend to stay unhappily caught in a hole with no exit. And that's no way to live your life.

Create the Necessary Reserves

Self-care is never a selfish act—it is simply good stewardship of the only gift I have.   **—PARKER PALMER**

Ruth works in a high-tech organization and is miserable. Her job requirements have changed and her position has become a terrible fit. She's hired me to help her find a new job. We worked on identifying her talents and interests and crafted a value proposition statement of what she has to offer. "The beauty of your employer is that it's huge," I said excitedly one day. "Armed with this statement, you can network like crazy and find another spot more suited to you!" "Well," replied Ruth, "I don't think I have the energy to do that."

Is Ruth crazy? Lazy? I don't think so. She's simply pointing to a truth: it *is* more effort to get out of her office and schmooze folks up as well as continue to do her current job.

That's one of the reasons learning to adapt is challenging. Because of the way our brains are structured, it takes a lot of energy to change. As I discussed earlier, the brain is designed to learn something, then to make it automatic to conserve energy. It was psychologist Donald Hebb who first identified in the late forties that in the brain, "cells that fire together wire together." As a child learning to tie your shoes, for instance, your brain cells fired in a certain sequence; as you practiced, the cells wired into a pathway that is now grooved into your brain. You don't have to think about tying your shoes and it takes hardly any energy at all.

I clearly remember being in this automatic mode for a time as the executive editor of Conari Press. We had a bestseller and soon were churning out book after book in the same format, selling them hand over fist. It was fun and easy. It was a rude awakening when it stopped working. Suddenly we had to sweat out and second-guess every detail from concept to cover to title to marketing. My brain was definitely more tired.

Because adapting takes more effort, we need to build up our energy reserves. Think of it as part of your job description as a Change Master. You simply must take care of yourself or you won't be able to cope.

That's why, with Ruth, rather than give her a rah-rah speech about how she needed to get out there and network, I offered her the following practice that we at PTP created after reading *The Power of Full Engagement* by Jim Loehr and Tony Schwartz. Loehr and Schwartz make the point that working people need to treat themselves like high-performance athletes do. Athletes have strategies for extending themselves (i.e., lifting weights) and strategies for recovery as well (i.e., resting). To have maximum energy, we need extension and recovery strategies in all the domains of our existence: physical, mental, emotional, and spiritual. The worksheet on page 131 gives you a snapshot of where you are right now and points to where you might want to go.

Here's what you do. In each domain—physical, mental,

emotional, and spiritual—think about what you're doing that is stretching you in that place and what you do to recover. Write them in the boxes on the right. Then rate yourself on a scale of 1 to 10 in the spaces on the left on how well you're doing in each, with 1 being very low and 10 being extremely high.

For instance, my physical-extension strategies are swimming in the summer and doing thirty minutes on the elliptical the rest of the year. I give myself a 5 (probably not enough extension, since I don't do it every day). For physical recovery, I sit in the hot tub, lie down and read a novel, and sleep eight to nine hours at night. I give myself an 8 (hitting it most days). Mentally, I am exerting myself writing a new book, coming up with ideas to help my clients, and dealing with a child going through puberty. I rate myself at 7. For recovery, I sit in the hot tub, lie down and read, and sleep eight to nine hours a night. (See a pattern?) I give myself an 8. Emotionally, I'm exerting myself trying not to give in to fear as the economy contracts. I'd rate it a 9. For recovery, I talk to friends, sit in the hot tub, and meditate. I'd give myself a 6. Spiritual can refer to religious practices or can be how you feel you are living your values and sense your connection to a larger whole. In spiritual extension, I would put meditating and practicing gratitude, and give myself a 4—I've got the gratitude practice down but rarely meditate. For spiritual recovery, I read uplifting books and talk with certain friends. A big 0 on that right now.

Your strategies will be different. That's okay. Just note them. A client of mine, for instance, swims every day as a physical-exertion strategy as well as a mental and emotional recovery one. There's no one right way.

Physical

YOUR STRATEGIES

How are you doing?

Extension:

1   10

Recovery:

1   10

Emotional

YOUR STRATEGIES

How are you doing?

Extension:

1   10

Recovery:

1   10

Mental

YOUR STRATEGIES

How are you doing?

Extension:

1   10

Recovery:

1   10

Spiritual

YOUR STRATEGIES

How are you doing?

Extension:

1   10

Recovery:

1   10

When Ruth did this, she discovered her extension numbers were very high and her recovery ones very low. She decided to go back to taking a yoga and meditation class, which she'd done in the past. That's helping her have the energy to get out and market herself into a new position.

Self-care isn't optional when we're riding the whitewaters of change. Make sure you're building up your reserves.

Don't Go into the Wilderness
Without Your Compass

This is our purpose: to make as meaningful as possible this life that has been bestowed upon us; to live in such a way that we may be proud of ourselves; to act in such a way that some part of us lives on.   —OSWALD SPENGLER

Joe has just gotten laid off. He tells me that he's been in this situation three times before. "What did you do those other times?" I asked. He proceeded to tell me what he'd done in each case, and a pattern began to emerge. Here's how he put it: "I get more in touch with what I love and how I want to contribute, and then I go out and convince someone to create a job for me doing that."

Without being fully aware of it, Joe is using his sense of purpose as a compass and that is a powerful navigational tool during change. Remember the 3Cs? One is commitment, which is another way of talking about purpose. Folks who are resilient get more in touch with their sense of purpose when faced with a change and look for ways to increase their sense of meaning in what they contribute. Great, you say, but I'm not sure what mine is or how to figure it out.

I think many of us are confused about this notion of purpose. We think it's a thunderbolt from the sky—you're supposed to cure world hunger!—that sets us off on a well-laid path from which we never deviate. It doesn't work like that, at least not for most of us. As Joseph Campbell said and I quote to my clients constantly, if you can see the path laid out before you, it is not yours. The path is always a mystery for the soul that is on it. In fact, it is the searching for the path and living into the mystery that is ours to do. Only in hindsight, when we look back, can we see the through line that we've created by our fumbling in the dark.

But there are ways to get closer to our sense of purpose. In her book *I Will Not Die an Unlived Life,* Dawna writes about how purpose is more like a constellation than a star. It's made up of four elements, which when taken together become the compass we can use to find our way in the unknown. It creates the acronym LIVE:

- L: What do I Love to do?

- I: What are my Inner talents?

- V: What are my Values? What really matters to me?

- E: What Environments bring out the best in me?

Harvard educator Howard Gardner discovered the importance of this compass when he researched people who had midcareer breakdowns. The questions people should be asking about work, he says, are: "Does this fit your values? Does it evoke excellence; are you highly competent and effective at what you do? Does it evoke . . . joy? . . . Decide what you really like to do and what you would like to spend your life doing. That's more important than deciding what particular job to hold, because the employment landscape is changing radically and quickly. Then ask, 'Where can I carry that out?' and be very flexible" about the possibilities.

When I work with people on this, I help them look at each element and then use them as a filtering system when they evaluate their options. In the next two chapters, you will have a chance to examine I and V. Here we'll look at L and E—what you love to do and what environments bring out the best in you. We'll use Marc as an example.

I ask Marc to make a list of what he loves to do (L). Here it is:

- bring people and ideas together; network
- start something from scratch
- partner with others
- create experiences

And here's his list for the environments that bring out his best (E):

- lots of autonomy and freedom but not working alone
- the chance to start something new
- having other people to execute the plan
- time alone

Do you notice an overlap? You'll probably see it in values and talents as well. There are often strong themes in common among the four elements, which I always take as a clue that you've touched the sweet spot of purpose.

Now it's your turn. When you list what you love, make sure you're naming things to do, not people. In environments, consider pacing, rhythm, people, activities that bring out your best.

Remember in the first section when I spoke about the differences beween your self and your behaviors! During times of change, you may be called on to take actions that you would prefer not to. But when you know what you love and the environments—the people, places, and other resources—that bring out the best in you, you can be sure to include those in your day, too, to give yourself the resilience to tackle the undesirable activities. For instance, I have to speak to someone I would rather not. So I am sure to take the time to read and sit in my hot tub, as those things bring out my best and enable me to adapt more effectively. Getting in touch with these things helps the light inside of me grow brighter, no matter what the outside world is asking of me. I strongly suggest that after you examine all four LIVE elements separately, you go back and look at the common themes. Ask yourself, "What does this say about my purpose and where I want to be heading now in my life?"

When Joe did that, it became clear to him that his purpose was to be found in creating opportunities for people and new ideas to come together through partnerships with others. He could do that online, he could do it through events planning, he could do it working for any number of organizations. He could do it in new product development, marketing, or communications. He's got a through line that has tremendous flexibility. That's what purpose creates, a compass that will help you orient without being too fixed in one direction.

"STAND BACK AND BE QUIET"

"The downturn has me refining everything," says Angelina, a construction company owner. "Rather than running around being reactive, I've slowed down and turned inward during the slowdown. I've used it as an opportunity to stand back and be quiet. To work on my spiritual development and personal growth. It's enabled me to respond more effectively to my husband, my employees, and my business."

What Are Your Inner Talents?

If human beings are perceived as potentials rather than problems, as possessing strengths instead of weaknesses, as unlimited rather than dull and unresponsive, then they thrive and grow to their capabilities. **—BOB CONKLIN**

Lisa's husband had to take a job in another state and she and her three kids can't move because they can't sell their house. So she has to learn to be a single parent, at least temporarily. "I'm worried about how I am going to do all the logistics. Like how to get out the door in the morning. I'm not good at that." "What about dealing with all the feelings—yours and the kids?" I asked. "Oh, that's easy," she replied.

Without knowing it, Lisa was telling me and herself something important about her inner talents, the I of her LIVE elements. There are many ways to think about talents but when we at PTP use the term, we're not talking about the ability to play an instrument or get the ball in the basket. We're talking about your talents in thinking, the habitual ways you approach problems. We all have different ones, which accounts for why two people can look at the exact same situation and see different aspects of it. Our dominant thinking helps determine what we're paying attention to in any situation.

When we get more in touch with what our talents in thinking are, we can use them even more consciously, train in them even more, and get even better at them, which research by the Gallup Organization has shown to increase our capacity for excellence.

PTP has created an assessment to determine your unique combination of thinking talents, called Thinking Talent cards, which you can find at www.ptp-partners.com. Here I'm going to have you focus on one aspect, what we call Domains of Competence. These describe four broad categories of thinking. Once you hear what they are, it's pretty easy for you to intuit which ones your mind typically uses. Research by Hermann International of a sample of two million people has found that 60 percent of us use two of these four, 30 percent use three, 6 percent use one, and only 4 percent use all four. They are as follows:

- Analytic: concerned with data, facts, numbers, being "logical" and rational. With money, concerned with ways to count. With time, concerned with the present.

- Procedural: concerned with processes, operationalizing, logistics, tactics. With money, concerned with ways to save. With time, concerned with the past, with how things have been done previously.

- Relational: concerned with feelings, morale, teamwork, helping people grow. With money, concerned with ways to help. Time isn't so important.

- Innovative: concerned with newness, possibilities, strategy, "big picture." With money, concerned with ways to spend to do exciting new things. With time, concerned with the future.

Notice your strongest domain(s). Which are your concerns in any given situation? Are you, like Ruth, energized by change, bored by numbers and routine, highly innovative, and have no use for "people problems"? She's one of the 6 percent of the population strong in just one domain. In her case, the Innovative one. Or are you more like Dan, great at numbers and following routines and highly uncomfortable with feelings and newness (Analytic and Procedural)? There is no right or wrong. Just notice what's true for you.

Notice also if there is one or more of these that you avoid. It's important to understand not only which one(s) are in your comfort zone but also which you don't typically use or even shy away from. We tend to worry in the place we don't have talents because somewhere inside we know we lack the required thinking.

That's why Lisa is worried about the logistics of the situation, where someone else might worry about the feelings part, for instance. She's strong in Relational thinking but not Procedural. You can use this information to determine, as you will discover in a later chapter, "Who Do You Need by Your Side?" who you may need to partner with to think your situation through. That's what Lisa did. She got a friend to help her create a morning system and has been able to follow it more or less, making her life much easier.

Right now, however, let's concentrate on your most dominant ways of thinking. These are the raw materials you bring to every situation you find yourself in. The more you put yourself in situations where they're needed, the better you'll be at the task. For instance, you probably don't want me to be the brainstorm person in product development, as I lack Innovative thinking. But I'm great at partnering with people who come up with the big ideas and helping them bring their ideas into reality with my Analytic, Procedural, and Relational talents. What about you?

Reexamine Your Priorities

You never want a serious crisis to go to waste. And what I mean by that is an opportunity to do things you think you could not do before.   **—RAHM EMANUEL, OBAMA'S CHIEF OF STAFF**

Alex was a high-flying investment guy who worked for Lehmann Brothers. So you know the end of the story. He's out of work and lost most of his money. Until this change, he'd led a life of privilege—big houses, boats, expensive cars and suits, business class every flight. He worked and played hard. Now he's stopped in his tracks. The question he keeps asking himself and everyone he sees is "What does this all mean?"

Alex has received what a spiritual teacher I know calls a life shock. A big fat boulder dropped out of the sky and knocked him flat. Everything he thought was important is now gone. It's left him questioning the meaning of life, as well as what up until now have been his largely unexamined priorities and values.

That reexamination is a good thing. That's why I love the opening quote by Rahm Emanuel. It's in alignment with what his boss, Barack Obama, made clear in the weeks after his election that he "sees the fiscal meltdown as a once-in-a-generation chance to reset the nation's priorities," as Zachary Coile paraphrased in the *San Francisco Chronicle.* One of the opportunities a monster wave of change always entails is a look at our priorities to see if and how they need to shift.

There are many ways to look at your priorities. You can look at where you spend your time, efforts, or money and think about how that should change. As challenges continue to rock the publishing world, a book publicist friend of mine did just that. "I looked at where I was spending my time," she said. "And I realized that I had a number of problematic authors who were taking a tremendous amount of my energy and time with their complaints and I wasn't getting a whole lot back in return. So I let them go and committed to working only with people I enjoy. If the money is going to be less, at least I can like the people I work for!"

But often, big changes initiate another kind of priority shift—which is more of a spiritual one, where you begin to ask yourself, "What really matters to me now? Given what's happened, how do I want to live now?" These are soul questions that can take those of us who are unfamiliar with them into uncharted waters. This is one of the gifts of unexpected change. It allows us to examine, perhaps for the very first time, the V of our LIVE elements, our values. And to reconnect—or finally connect—to what has the most meaning to us.

Once I was helping a client do a values clarification process—that I'm also going to invite you to do (see the "What Values Underlie the Choices You've Made in Your Life?" box)—in which you look at the decisions you made in your life and what values were represented by the choices you made. I've written about this exercise before, but I include it here because it's such a great way to get clear about your lived values. The decisions we make are the best indicators of the values we hold most dear. A decision is a choice for something and that something is a value of ours or we wouldn't choose it.

"What happens if you see that you've been choosing for all the wrong things?" my client asked plaintively once I explained the process. "Well," I replied, "if you allow the pain of that awareness to touch you not with shame or guilt but with the plain truth of it, then you can start to live from the values that matter to you now and make different choices from now on."

That's the process Alex is going through. Where it will lead him is too soon to say.

The other day I ran into an acquaintance and we

started talking about the challenges she's facing. She said, "It's hard, but it's also a chance to remember what really matters. Not the big car or the summer house or going out to dinner, but the beauty of simplicity and the joy connecting to loved ones and helping one another as much as you can. As much as I'm struggling to keep my business afloat, I'm appreciating the opportunity to remember what's truly important."

WHAT VALUES UNDERLIE THE CHOICES YOU'VE MADE IN YOUR LIFE?

Take out a large piece of paper. At the bottom draw a small V like two branches of a tree. (See my example on page 143.) Think about the first major decision you made on your own. For me it was what college to go to. Write down the two choices, one on each branch. For me it came down to Cornell or Brandeis. In the middle of the V write the value represented by your choice. I chose Cornell and picked it for prestige and weather (false advertising, but . . .). Then off the branch you chose, draw another V for the next major choice and think about the decision and what you were choosing for. Keep on going until you have a tree of your choices, with the values that you used to choose. Then make a list of those values. If you've chosen for love twenty times, write *love* twenty times. It will show you how much you value it. What does the list tell you about what has mattered to you? Are they the same things that matter now? What values do you want to choose with from now on?

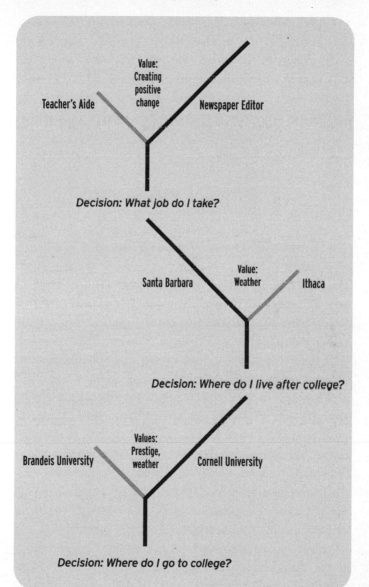

Value:
Creating
positive
change

Teacher's Aide   Newspaper Editor

Decision: What job do I take?

Santa Barbara   Value: Ithaca
                       Weather

Decision: Where do I live after college?

Values:
Prestige,
weather

Brandeis University   Cornell University

Decision: Where do I go to college?

Oprah Winfrey wrote recently in *O* that "We need a shift in the way we think about our lives. We may have to search deeply to recognize what matters. Sometimes when I ask people what it would take to make them happy, they don't know what to say." I hope that no matter what else this change brings, it is accompanied by a greater awareness of your unique answer to Oprah's question.

Envision Your Next Chapter

Pain pushes until vision pulls.

—ANONYMOUS

Monica's family business went under a few months ago. At first, she was grateful for a chance to get out of the rat race of work, but she's now having trouble getting into motion again. "I don't know what's wrong with me," she confided, "I just feel like giving up and hiding in a hole for the next ten years. What's going on?"

Monica is in the midst of a transition brought on by an unasked-for change. When this happens, one chapter of our lives has come to a close and a new one is about to begin. The uncomfortable gap in between, when we may feel malaise or even panic, is the transition. It doesn't usually feel so good, but recognizing what's going on can help alleviate a bit of the discomfort. So can viewing your life as a book with many chapters.

I learned this perspective from Candice Carpenter, one of the founders of iVillage, among many other accomplishments, in her book *Chapters*. Because we're all living longer and change is accelerating, we will go through many chapters, each with its own dramas, excitement, requirements, and difficulties. Just like with a great novel, we may not be sure where the story will take us and can feel lost or confused.

I love Carpenter's approach because it helps us make sense of our lives as a whole, and encourages us to seek the narrative of our lives beneath the surface of our day-to-day activities. It provides the long view. When I work with people like Monica who are reeling from a change not of their choosing, I ask them to go back through their lives and name the chapters they've lived so far, to give them titles just like in a book. Then, in order to help them get their future thinking going, I ask them what they'd like the next chapter to be called. That's important because, as the opening quote says, "pain pushes until vision pulls." The more we're connected to what we want to go toward in our lives, the more energy and enthusiasm we have to make the journey. But remember, just like in a book, you usually don't know exactly what's in the next chapter until you've lived it. That's what makes life so exciting—and challenging!

Monica spent some time thinking about the chapters in her life so far and what they say about what matters to her. It helped her realize that she has always been passionate about the environment but has never had a chance to fully live that commitment in her work. Having gotten in touch with a possible future that excites her, she's named the next chapter in her life "My Green Thumb" and is in the process of looking for a job in an environmental field that will make that title a reality.

Go back and give the chapters of your life titles. Then

look at the pattern. What do you want the name of your next chapter to be? There should be some sense of excitement when you say it. That's a clue that you're in touch with some real desire.

This is no idle exercise. I did it when I turned fifty and noticed how much work and effort my life had contained up to that point. So I named the next chapter "Easy Does It." And so far at least, my fifties have in fact been the most effortless decade of my life.

You are not just at the mercy of outside forces. Change always creates a death and the possibility of rebirth. Your life has a trajectory that is created from some mysterious combination of outside pressures and internal longings. It's part of our job as Change Masters to not just rotely bend ourselves into whatever shape seems to be called for, but to use the pressure to become more of who we are and to offer more of what we have to give.

Who Do You Need by Your Side?

Our tendency to create heroes rarely jibes with the reality that most nontrivial problems require collective solutions.

—WARREN G. BENNIS

Whenever I get scared about the future, which is often, I remember one thing about myself: I am good at partnering with other people. And the best partners for me are people who are great at innovative thinking. To put it simplistically, they provide the what, the idea of where we need to go; I provide the how, the steady elbow grease of doing it. As I described earlier, Innovative thinking is not my strongest suit. But what's required in change is a tremendous amount of Innovative thinking, so I would be up the creek without a paddle if I didn't partner with those who are good at it.

I was thinking about this recently when I read an article in the *Gallup Management Journal* by Rodd Wagner and Gale Muller. They'd just completed five years of research on partnerships. In it they quoted *Forbes* publisher Rich Karlgaard: "Build on your strengths. To mitigate your weaknesses—and we all have them—partner up. Find your complement."

Never is this advice more pertinent than when you're adapting to changing circumstances. Unfortunately, say Wagner and Muller, their research shows that people are "partnership-poor." "The most common number of work partnerships . . . is zero. Asked if they have *ever* had a great partnership at work, about one quarter of employees say no." This is a problem, they say, because "[e]ven one strong collaborative relationship markedly increases your well-being over those who are going it alone."

I couldn't agree more. Here's why: You've already discovered your Domains of Competence in "What Are Your Inner Talents?" Since only 4 percent of us have talent in all four, we all have blind spots where we need support, particularly now, when we need to adapt swiftly. You may, like me, need a partner who's good at envisioning the future. Or some other kind of thinking. The head of a small construction company I know who's great at doing the work but terrible at time and money management just partnered with a person who's great at project management, which falls in the Procedural domain.

One client of mine who's been an incredibly successful solo contributor at a high-tech company just got a promotion that involves managing a team of fifteen. Not only does she not have any experience with managing people, she doesn't have any Relational thinking talents. Her natural management style would be to tell them to go away, work hard, and leave her alone. Fortunately, she recognizes her gap and has come to me for support. I can teach her tools and techniques, but I'm not there with her every day. So my first suggestion is to find someone on her team who's great at Relational thinking to partner with. She's already on the search.

TIPS FOR FINDING THE RIGHT PARTNER

- Make sure your partner is not in conflict with what you're trying to do. For example, the change you're going through might feel risky for a spouse, so he or she might unthinkingly sabotage it.

- Make sure they help you move forward, not help you stay stuck. Often we get together to complain and think that's taking action. Complaining is okay, as long as it's not all you do together.

- Depending on your situation and who you are, you might need different partners to provide different things—a person to provide encouragement, a person to think through options with, a person to help you stay accountable for what you said you'd do.

What kind of person or persons do you need to partner with? What kind of thinking is not habitual for you? You want someone, as the *Forbes* publisher pointed out, to complement your thinking. After you've found someone comes the hard part: respecting and learning from the other person rather than letting them drive you crazy. Remember, you're partners because you each offer something the other doesn't have. Make sure you take advantage of the differences. It will give you an advantage in adapting. And don't get discouraged if it takes you a while to find the right person.

Watch the Road, Not the Potholes

The longer we dwell on our misfortunes, the greater is their power to harm us. —VOLTAIRE

Lana Calloway is president of Exhibit Resources, a company that does design, construction, and installation of trade-show exhibits. Following the 9/11 terrorist attacks, Lana and many of her clients were forced to cut staff. She noticed that coordinating details for trade shows was overwhelming for many clients who had slashed their marketing budgets. So Lana's company began offering turn-key trade-show project-management services, and her business has since boomed. Her story is the perfect example of how in every crisis lies an opportunity.

That attitude can be hard for some of us because we're focused on the problem, not the potential. Take me, for instance. I come from the school of "dwell on your worries obsessively and they won't happen or at least they won't be as bad as when you ignore them." Sound familiar? Over the past dozen years or so, I've been working on changing that thought pattern because it doesn't seem to produce anything but more anxiety, which I can do without. Still, when change scares me, I find my mind going straight to all that I don't want to happen, rather than what I do.

I was reminded once again about the danger of this behavior while reading *The Unthinkable*. In it, author Amanda Ripley describes a phenomenon called potholism: "the more drivers stare at potholes, the more likely they are to drive into them." Rather than concentrating on avoiding a pothole, says Ronn Langford of driving school MasterDrive, you should focus on the whole road so you can see where to drive.

What a message for us all! Focusing on the problems or anticipated problems of change will cause us to drive right toward them. Rather, we should expand our vision so that we are seeing the whole situation and focus on what we want out of the new situation, not what we don't.

One of the reasons this lesson is so important is that under fear, our senses narrow—we get tunnel vision, hearing, and feeling. It's part of that old fight-or-flight mechanism. Our perceptions narrow so that we focus only on the danger. But as Langford's driving research shows, this can be dangerous in and of itself, causing us to head toward the problem rather than away from it. When we widen our focus and expand our peripheral vision, we tell that primitive part of our brains there's no danger and it turns off, leaving us more able to think fully about the situation.

There's another reason why focusing on the road instead of the hole is important. It's got to do with what *The Secret* is about. Say what you will about that massive bestseller, but there is a kernel of truth there as far as I understand. We all have the ability to use our energy in three ways—dynamically, to create the forward momentum of action; receptively, to become aware of what is available around and within us; and magnetically, to draw toward us that which we're powerfully pulling in. *The Secret* is referring to magnetic energy, the attracting of what we persistently focus on.

Fear is a powerful attractor because we imagine a bad outcome so vividly in our minds, usually without knowing it. We make a scary movie complete with sound, lights, and action, which creates a strong pull on exactly what we don't want, like the pothole. That's how we may unconsciously contribute to a bad thing happening. Notice I said *may contribute,* not cause. There are many other very powerful factors—social, environmental, political—which are beyond our control that are powerfully influencing our lives. So don't use this logic to beat yourself up if something bad occurs.

But because I want to increase my odds of success in as many ways as possible, I make it a practice to consciously give my attention to what I *do* want in a situation, not what I don't, so magnetic energy will be on my side.

How about you? Think about what you want, the best outcome to the situation. Now, vividly imagine the best result coming to pass—see, feel, and hear yourself in the experience. That's what Olympic athletes do. Psychologist Stephen Ungerleider, who serves on the U.S. Olympic Committee Sports Psychology Registry, found that 83 percent of athletes surveyed used some form of positive mental imagery. Why shouldn't you?

Take a minute when you wake up each morning and just before you go to sleep at night to bring to your mind the vivid positive outcome you want—a good new job, a product that sells, a partner to help. Make it as colorful, loud, and real to yourself as possible. Imagine that you have a fishing rod in your hand. Throw that line out and hook that thing you want and reel it in. You'll be using your magnetic energy to help attract what you want. During the day, every time you catch yourself focusing on the pothole, simply substitute your best possible result. It may not cause a miracle to occur, but I guarantee it will help make avoiding that big pothole a bit easier.

STEP 3: TAKE ACTION

Don't wait for something big to occur. Start where you are, with what you have, and that will always lead you into something greater. —MARY MANIN MORRISSEY

Now it's time to get into action based on the options you've brainstormed and what you've learned about your passions, talents, values, and best environments. This section is about making a plan and getting into motion, evaluating your progress, and revising as needed along the way. It includes chapters on the attitudes and behaviors that will hold you in good stead as you get into the action phase of AdaptAbility. You'll learn why the 80 percent solution is so important, why it's good to try several things at once, why you should adopt the attitude of an improv actor, and why revision is such a crucial skill. Hopefully the actions you take and the course corrections you make will not only help you feel more in control, but will soon find you thriving in your new circumstances.

Create a Story of Possibility

Adversity causes some men to break; others to break records. —WILLIAM A. WARD

I was working with Arlene, whose husband had died in middle age. It was several years later and she had not moved on because she truly believed that his death had ruined her life. "I always imagined that we'd be together in old age, and he went and ruined everything," she complained to me. "No one wants to include a widow in parties. I'm going to be lonely for the rest of my life. Why did this terrible thing happen to me?"

As you learned in early chapters, our brains are constantly taking what happens to us and making meaning out of it. In a certain way, each of us is a master storyteller. When change brings us challenges we must adapt to, perhaps in ways that we would prefer not to have to, we have a choice. We can tell ourselves a story like, "I have to move in with my sister. My entire life is doomed, it will be like this forever, it's all my fault." Or something like, "Moving in with my sister is hard, but there are still things I can enjoy and appreciate about my life; it's only temporary; it's something that's happening to lots of people."

As Martin Seligman points out in his book *Learned Optimism,* the first is a story with three dangerous Ps: pervasiveness (it's ruined everything in my life), permanence (it will be like this forever), and personal (I am the sole person going through this terrible thing, it's all my fault). When we tell ourselves such stories, we easily fall into despair. We get stuck and find it harder to adapt, if we can at all. Like Arlene, we become full of bitterness and resentment, cold forms of anger that poison our present and stop us from creating a positive future.

The second kind of story turns those three Ps on their head. It reminds us that while the situation is challenging, there are still wonderful aspects to our lives (nonpervasive), that circumstances can change (impermanent), and it's not happening only to you (impersonal). It activates another P, one that we need at our side as we adapt: possibility. It's what makes the difference between whether adversity breaks us or helps us break records. Dawna calls the first kind a rut story because it's like a broken record that keeps us stuck, and the second a river story because it carries us to new possibilities.

I explained to Arlene about the two kinds of stories and challenged her to come up with a river story about her circumstances that she could believe in. I told her the story had to have the same exact circumstances in it, but with a different interpretation. At first she couldn't do it at all. She was convinced that her version of reality was simply the truth. But as we worked together, she began to open her mind. Nothing was different except how she was talking to herself about her circumstances. But that helped her begin to enjoy her life a bit more. After a short while, we ended our work.

This week, out of the blue, an e-mail entitled "Telling Stories" arrived from her. It read: " 'Story 1: My husband died and I am too uncomfortable to call a friend so I am taking a bus alone with strangers to DC to see a museum. Story 2: I've always envied women who travel alone and have new experiences. So I'm going to take a bus alone with new people to DC to explore a museum I've wanted to see.' I'm doing good, aren't I?"

Now it's your turn. What story do you choose to tell yourself about the adapting you're doing right now? Make sure it's a river story with the right P—possibility. Here's what a client said to me about looking for a job: "It's a hard time right now to get a job because of the downturn.

But my situation is only temporary. I'm going to work hard on looking and not worry for three months because with unemployment I've got enough money to last that long. I'm sure something will come along, I've got a lot of connections."

Stories of possibility keep us thinking creatively and productively as we adapt. Keep yours handy so if you find your mind drifting to the negative Ps, you can stop and tell yourself a more useful story. It's a strategy that creates Change Masters.

GET TIME ON YOUR SIDE

Because it's important not to get stuck feeling that your situation is permanent, it's important to figure out what time horizon is best suited for you and your change. "I could never do the 'one day at a time' thing," says Roger, "because that would never allow me to actually adapt to doing this job that I don't like. What works best for me is to tell myself that I'm doing this for six months and then will reassess. It's a long enough time for me to adapt to the situation, but not so long that I feel I am stuck forever." What's true for you? Many people do well with one day at a time: "I can put up with my annoying boss until five o'clock when I can work on my résumé." Or a week: "I'm going to focus on doing a good job this week and not think beyond that." Others, like Roger, need longer frames. What time horizon will give you the most comfort and ease?

Make Deposits into Your Hope Account

There has never been anything false about hope.

—BARACK OBAMA

For years, Martha worked in a nonprofit and loved it. Eventually, however, she realized she wanted to run an organization, not just work for one. So she quit in midlife and got an MBA, returning to the workforce just as jobs dried up. Now what? She couldn't find work so, in her fifties, she ended up moving in with her parents and helping as her dad died and her mother slipped away due to Alzheimer's. But she never gave up hope of running her own foundation for kids who can't afford art and music education, and as a result, she continued to talk about it wherever she went.

Then, on a plane flight, she was seated next to a guy who turned out to be a wealthy philanthropist who got so excited about her idea that he's agreed to fund it completely. These days, Martha's busy putting the organization together, grateful that she had continued to hope, to not let her dream slip away.

In Greek mythology, when Pandora opened the box and let out all the troubles that have since plagued the world, she also let out a tiny fairy who said, "Yes, it is true that you have unleashed all manner of afflictions upon the world, but you have also let me out. I am Hope and will always be there to bring hope to humans, whenever they are in trouble."

The Greeks were onto something. This myth goes to the

heart of the truth that it's difficult to endure hardships without hope. Hope offers balm for the soul in the moment and encouragement to keep on going. Recently, positive psychology has begun to explore this quality. Psychologist Shane Lopez conducts research and training in the role of hope in our daily lives. He says that hope is "the ideas and energy you have for the future. . . . It forms when goal thinking (I want to go from here to there) combines with pathways thinking (I know many ways to get from here to there), and agency thinking (I think I can get from here to there)." His research has shown a strong correlation between hope and a sense of well-being and has demonstrated that people can learn how to be more hopeful.

What do you want to make happen in the situation you find yourself in now? Hope helps you vote for the best outcome with your imagination as well as with your feet, in terms of taking action. Like all the other positive emotions, it actually helps you be more creative and resourceful in your thinking. (According to research by psychologist Barbara Frederickson, positive emotions make you more aware of what's happening and improves your capacity to notice details and perform tasks.) And hope increases your ability to endure difficulties and persist in the face of setbacks.

A few years ago, I met one of the world's experts on stress, Dr. Pamela Peeke. She's an expert at adapting and adjusting; one of her favorite sayings is "It is what it is," which is a great one for quickly passing the acceptance stage of adaptation. She's the person who did the research on the stress-fat connection and introduced me to the work of the father of stress research, Dr. Hans Selye.

Selye, says Dr. Peeke, discovered that stress is simply

part of life—the natural result of an organism bumping up against an ever-changing environment to which it must adapt. What's dangerous, he discovered, was what he called dis-stress, feeling hopeless, helpless, and defeated in the face of those changes. That's similar to what the resiliency experts I referred to earlier found—that the more control we take in a situation and the deeper positive meaning we give to it, the better off we are because we stay out of helplessness and defeat.

What I'd like to highlight here is the importance of hope as you adapt. It's the energy you need to put your plan into action and keep swimming as long as it takes to get to the shore. Selye found that if he stressed rats over and over (kind of what you may feel is happening to you right now), they began to exhibit signs of chronic distress. But when after stressing them he held and petted them, the nurturing reversed the stress symptoms. As Dr. Peeke wrote in an article on body-mind medicine, "The gentle touching transformed the animal's perception of hopelessness, helplessness, and defeat into one of hope. The neuropeptides of hope [meaning the feel-good hormones that are released when we experience a positive emotion] flowed through the body's network, modulating and potentially eliminating the toxicity of the physical stress."

As you adapt, you need to hope for the best outcome. What gives you hope? How can you increase your hope account right now? I do it by remembering that I've made it so far, thinking of all the people in my life that I can count on for help if needed, and reading inspirational stories of people who have overcome hardships to make a difference. What about you?

"I THOUGHT YOU JUST PLODDED ON"

"I've always been pretty good at doing what needed to be done," says Sarah. "But I always focused on the dark side. I marched on, dragging the baggage of unasked-for change behind me: it wasn't fair that I was adopted, that my parents were alcoholics, that my fiancé left me, that I had to move. The list went on and on. I thought you just plodded on accumulating sorrow. It never occurred to me that change could be good until I was finally diagnosed with depression and received proper treatment. Now it's possible for me to focus on the positive side of change. To see all that I have developed in myself as a result of the things I've gone through, as well as the good things that have come from the changes in my life including a wonderful husband and children I never would have had if my fiancé hadn't dumped me. I'm able to focus on the benefits of adapting and finally left my baggage behind me. How freeing!"

If you have lost all hope and are feeling hopeless, helpless, and defeated by your situation or if you feel suicidal, please, please seek professional help immediately—a therapist, support group, hotline, or clergy member. Depression and despair is an all-too-real condition that saps energy and creates immobility. You can't adapt well and create a positive future in that state of being. Hope is one of the energies you need to cope.

Hope Is Not a Plan

He that lives upon hope will die fasting.

—BENJAMIN FRANKLIN

A friend was telling me about how her husband, Jeff, a free-lance designer, hasn't had any new projects for a year. "In the past," she said, "someone always came to his rescue and found him something. So he has hope that will happen again. But hope is not a plan!"

What an important truth—hope is not a plan, as Benjamin Franklin also alludes to in the opening quote. We need the energy of hope as an emotional buoy and the biology of hope to repair our minds and bodies from the ravages of stress. But we need more than hope or else we're stuck in wishful thinking. Wishful thinking is dangerously irresponsible because it keeps us from action: "Somehow this problem will go away and my life will be a bed of roses. I don't have to actually do anything to help my wish along." Yes, we need hope. But we also need a plan.

So, now that you've expanded your options, it's time to articulate your plan. How are you going to adapt to this change? Make it as concrete as possible—"look for another job" is not a plan because it doesn't have action attached. You must know what actions you're going to take: update your résumé, call everyone you know, look on job websites, go to industry events, etc.

People make this crucial mistake all the time. I'm working with an organization in which people are creating learning plans for coping with the changes in their industry. Each person had to write three things they were going to do. Here are two examples of what they came up with: "get better at coaching my team"; "build a better business focus." See the problem? They don't have an action attached. How are they going to get better at these things? These are aspirations, not a plan of action. If you don't know the how, you don't have a plan that is worth anything. In fact, it's less than worthless because you think you're doing something when you're actually not.

As I wrote in *This Year I Will . . .*, to create success you need a plan with SMART actions. SMART stands for:

- **S**pecific: you know what the action is

- **M**easurable: you can tell when you've done it

- **A**chievable: it's possible to do

- **R**elevant: it relates to the problem at hand and matters to you

- **T**ime bound: there's a deadline attached

Once I taught them, my two clients mentioned above changed their aspirations into SMART goals: "to get better at coaching my team by partnering with Stan, who's great at it, and sitting in on the development conversations he's having with his people over the next month and watching how he does it"; "to build a better business focus by taking a course on the fundamentals of finance for managers the first quarter of 2009."

Here's another example. Oscar's company is planning

layoffs in the next month, and his goal is to keep his job. Here's his SMART goal: "I am going to increase my odds by launching the e-newsletter the boss has been wanting within a week while keeping up all my other work." It's specific (he's going to create an e-newsletter); measurable (when it exists, he's done it); achievable (it's possible to do); relevant (the boss has been wanting it and our guy cares about keeping his job); and time-bound (he's doing it in a week).

So now it's your turn. Be sure that you are SMART with what you're going to do. Know what success means so you know when you've gotten there. With some things, cutting debt, for instance, that's easy. It's when you're at zero. But for other changes, getting more customers, for instance, you need to challenge yourself to create measures of success. How many more? And keep the time lines short— don't make a plan that takes three months to see if it's getting you closer to what you want.

When you are ready to move forward, stop and make sure you've created a SMART goal. It's a crucial tool for creating the success you want.

Get the Balls in the Air

We immediately become more effective when we decide to change ourselves rather than asking things to change for us.

—STEPHEN COVEY

I'm working with two people in the same large company. It's in tremendous flux—the division they are in has reorganized something like six times in the last two years. (I call that chaos, not organization!) Theoretically, I am doing the same thing with each of them—helping them build their brand and find a spot using their talents within the changing organization. But the conversations go very differently.

Maia reports in each time with a list of actions she's taken since our last call. She's clear on her brand and is reaching out to as many people as she can to let them know what she's good at and what she's looking for. She's now choosing between several offers as people within her company vie for her talents.

Larry, on the other hand, is not getting the same results. He's not comfortable pursuing several avenues at once. He keeps looking at the company's internal job board, applying for a particular job, and waiting till he finds out if he got it to apply for the next one.

In terms of the Domains of Competence, Larry has a lot of Procedural thinking, which is very step by step; and Maia, a lot of Innovative, which is comfortable with simultaneous action. Unfortunately for Larry, the times we live in don't allow a lot of time for sequential action. It just takes too long. Company rumors are that a hiring freeze is on the way, which, if true, would mean that Larry would be out of luck. Rather than change his behavior to suit the times, Larry insists on doing it his same old way, possibly to his detriment.

Whether you naturally *think* sequentially or not, chances are you can't afford to *do* things sequentially right now. Things are just moving too fast and are too much in flux to pursue one course of action to its end before beginning to try something else. Simultaneity creates an advantage because when you have more than one ball in the air, you increase your chances that something will come of at least one of them.

Take Luis, for example, who just had to shut down his online business. He's applying for jobs in companies while reaching out to offer consulting services to the contacts he generated through his previous business. Even if he lands a

WHERE SHOULD YOU BE SPENDING YOUR TIME?

This is an example from a marketing model, but it can apply to any situation where you need to exert efforts in several directions at once. Imagine you are a project manager for a small food company and have been laid off. The easiest thing is to (1) market yourself to a competitor doing what you've already done. So most of your time (and money, if it applies) should be spent there. Harder is to (2) market yourself in a different area (like project management for a health care company instead of a food one). Hardest is to (3) change companies and fields (e.g., doing product design for tech companies). So you want to exert most efforts on 1, some on 2, and less but not none on 3. After all, you may need to switch careers altogether. Your actions for option 3 may be finding out more about the field, what training is required, and what the opportunities are rather than applying for jobs, which is what you would be doing in 1. For 2, you might be networking and asking people what it takes to make such a switch. Make sure you act on all three, but with the right actions and amount of effort for each.

full-time job, chances are he can continue to offer consulting on the side, thus giving him more income and a measure of stability if he ends up getting laid off.

That's why I suggest to folks, whatever their issue is, to try to take several actions simultaneously—look for work in a company and try a home business. Or search for a distributor for your products while developing an online strategy, for example. Look at renting your house at the same time as selling it. Try fertility treatments and look into adoption.

You can't be single-minded in the things you're trying. You want to explore the options and do something across a spectrum in parallel, not sequentially. For help considering how much time to spend in each area, see the "Where Should You Be Spending Your Time?" box.

To make sure you're pursuing enough options, return to your goal and make sure that it includes SMART actions across a spectrum. If you don't naturally think in parallel, find help from someone who does. Realize that it might feel awkward to you. Now you know why—it's just not your natural way of thinking. Ask yourself what help you will need in thinking in parallel.

That's what I did with Larry. Once I explained what he was doing and how it wasn't serving him, he figured out that he needed a lot of practice pitching himself, even when there wasn't a specific job at stake. He rehearsed with me and several friends and has now begun to network more effectively within his organization; he's even heard of a possibility that would fit him perfectly.

Think Through the Implications

Good plans shape good decisions.

—LESTER R. BITTEL

Gail was asked to swap roles with a colleague, Brenda. "Okay," I said, "what are the implications of that?" "Well," said Gail, "Brenda and I will still have to work together a lot and need to have a good relationship. She's very competitive, so I'm concerned that once I get in the role and make changes, she'll get defensive and start badmouthing me to the boss." "Okay," I replied, "let's make a plan to minimize that possibility." Gail ended up pursuing a strategy of offering to help Brenda get oriented, asking Brenda's help in return and praising in public what she genuinely could of the job Brenda had done. So far the change is going smoothly.

Often when we're faced with a change, we're so focused on the big thing—in Gail's case, doing a great job—that we don't take the time to think through the implications of what's happening—for Gail, working with a competitive colleague—and how best to respond. But it's an important step.

"Whenever people come to me to help them think about a new role at work," explains my colleague Esther, "I always ask them to pretend they are already doing the job. To imagine what they will actually be doing. It's one thing to decide something in the abstract. It's another to get down in the weeds of it." Otherwise you may end up like all those folks I've read about who decided to become teachers after leaving the business world. They went through the training and lasted only a year in the classroom because the reality was so different from their imaginings. You want to be as prepared as possible for what you're getting into.

So try it on, as my friend Patrick says. Think as specifically as possible about what you're going to do. For instance, if you no longer can send your child to a private school, what does that mean? Where will he go? How will you help him cope with the transition? Can you help him find someone to show him the ropes? Meet some kids in advance?

The more explicit you get in running through scenarios and deciding how you'll adapt, the less upset, angry, or frustrated you'll be in the actual situation. You won't be caught off guard once the reality occurs. Like Gail, you may be able to anticipate and head off problems in advance.

Can you anticipate everything? Of course not. That's why ongoing AdaptAbility is so crucial. But the more you anticipate, the more prepared you'll be.

Just Do One Thing

The secret of getting ahead is getting started. The secret of getting started is breaking your complex, overwhelming tasks into small, manageable ones, then starting on the first one.

—MARK TWAIN

Annie is a great planner. She's looking for work and has an action list as long as her arm. "The problem is that I look at it and get overwhelmed," she confided to me the other day. "Then I start to worry I'll never get work and it drives me right to bed. Or to tears. Help!"

Change can feel overwhelming, particularly if what you must do has a lot of actions or a tight time frame. That's why I suggest that after you make a plan, you break it down into small, manageable pieces and then look at just the next step or action. For instance, I am writing this book on a tight deadline. If I say to myself, "I have to do this whole thing in eight weeks," I freak out, which prevents me from doing the task itself. So I figured out how much I had to write each day to meet the deadline and then I purposely didn't look at the whole, just the next step: write four chapters today, for instance. Because that feels doable, I stay out of panic. It's also a way of experiencing success—hurrah, I did four!—which creates encouragement to keep on going.

Some things can't be broken into smaller tasks. But you can still use the principle of doing just the next thing rather than looking at the whole. That's what I suggested to Annie. "Your job is not to find a job, but to send out three e-mails a day to contacts you have and to respond if anyone e-mails you back," I said. "Does that feel doable?" She said yes and went off to do it. I gave her one other task: to stop and appreciate herself for doing those three e-mails a day.

"It's much better," she enthused a couple of weeks later. "I've made so much more progress this way. In fact, many days I've done more than three. And I've gotten a couple leads to follow."

How can you break your plan down or focus on just the

one small task? The more you put it into bite-sized pieces, the easier it will feel. As Friedrich Engels put it, "An ounce of action is worth a ton of theory." And remember the power of support in making the task easier. When I was packing up to move after my (unasked-for) divorce, a friend volunteered to come when I got to the kitchen. She knew that it would be the hardest room to pack because cooking was a time when my husband and I bonded. Plus there was a lot of stuff to go through. Her presence was incredibly helpful, as was taking it one cabinet at a time.

Think through what intermediate steps are involved in order to take the next step. For instance, you're out of work and decide to go to a networking event Friday. That means having an up-to-date résumé, an elevator speech about what you're looking for, and something to wear. Or you decide to stop eating in restaurants and cook more at home. You need to know what you're going to cook, buy the food, and budget the time. People get tripped up regularly on these details and allow precious time to drift by. Challenge yourself to think ahead to what's needed and to do those intermediate steps ASAP.

As the proverb goes, slow and steady wins the race. You can do what needs to be done, one small step after another. And be kind to yourself if some days you don't even manage that one thing. Rather than judging, blaming, or shaming yourself, which just keeps you stuck, ask yourself, "I wonder what would make it easier for me to do this tomorrow. When did I do it well? What were the circumstances?" That way you discover your formula of success and can follow it again: "When I did it last time, I woke up, read an inspirational passage in my daily meditation book, then got into action right away. I can do that tomorrow!"

> ## "I'VE BEEN DOWN THIS ROAD BEFORE"
>
> "Last month I found myself with no income," said Bonnie. "I've been down this road before when I lost everything and had to start all over. I asked myself what I did last time. It was two things: First, I embraced the bad feeling. I commiserated with myself and let myself cry as long as I wanted. Then I made a plan and took action—whether I felt like it or not. That's key. First to indulge my feelings and then to ignore them. If I waited to act until I felt like it, I wouldn't do anything."

Ready, Fire, Aim

We've all become great innovators on behalf of our companies and our work environments. Now we need to turn that spirit of radical innovation to our own lives.   —CANDICE CARPENTER

I once read an article on the actor Don Cheadle. He said he'd studied jazz in order to become a better actor because it's so much about improvisation. Hmm, I thought. Then two friends took an improv theater workshop to get better at their jobs. "People who succeed in this economy are the ones who can improvise the fastest," said one.

But I really got the message when I received an e-mail out of the blue from Katie Goodman. Katie is, among other things, an improv comedian and creativity coach who's written a book called *Improvisation for the Spirit.* I bet if it had been published a bit later, it might be titled *Improvisation for Hard Times,* because it certainly is a skill we could all use right now.

I'm not saying you have to become an improvisational comedian (although given what we're all going through, it might not be a bad idea!). Rather, I'm suggesting that we get more in tune with the spirit of improvisation, which is all about working with what shows up and not seeing mistakes as mistakes, but as the next thing to riff off of. To be swift on your feet when changes strike, that's the goal of improv. Some of Katie's chapters—"Be Present & Aware," "Be Open and Flexible," "Take Risks," "Trust," "Surrender"— sound like qualities we all need to cultivate.

In one chapter, she writes about website designer David Thompson, who talks about how to become creatively nimble. "[Y]ou have to [act] in a ready, fire, aim sort of way," he says. "You can't perfect something before it goes out on the Internet, because you don't know how it will work. You have to fire it out, get some feedback, and then re-aim it."

That's exactly what we need to do when we're in the action phase of the change cycle. We make a plan, then get into action and see what happens. This helps us stay out of analysis paralysis. You don't need to wait until you have the "perfect" plan. An 80 percent solution is better than no action at all. Think of it as an experiment. You're going to try something and see how it works. Based on your results, you will respond and revise.

When we adopt the spirit of improv, the action, evaluation, and respond process goes quickly because we don't spend time in indecision (Should I do it?"); rumination ("Why can't or won't I do it?"); or regret ("Oh, I just blew it."). We just do and keep on doing, responding to the bounce back we get. The key is to adjust based on the feedback—don't get caught in the trap of continuing to do the same thing expecting different results.

Taylor figured this out for herself as she struggled to deal with the downturn of her home business. "I've always been the one creating year-long plans, five-year plans. So the biggest thing about adapting I've learned is to get more comfortable with not knowing that far out. To keep my focus on the short term—this month and next, not where we'll be in a year, because you can't know that. I'm using less force and more positioning, developing more patience and acceptance. It's like I'm concentrating on building one brick at a time rather than the whole house."

Katie quotes an experienced improv actor who says that, with experience, you can get so interested in this process of responding to what happens that you "aren't affected by the quality of the show . . . equally interested in a 'good' or 'bad' or 'mediocre' show . . . that's the goal. To be equally excited by all of it. The whole process." Wouldn't it be great if we could feel that way about our lives? How much less stress, anxiety, and worry would we live without?

I can't say I'm there yet, when it comes to being equally excited no matter what happens. But I do try to embody the spirit of improv when it comes to getting into action, getting feedback, and quickly revising. One of the ways you can put that into effect with the change you're dealing

> ### GIVE YOURSELF A GOLD STAR!
>
> It's crucially important that you celebrate your small successes along the way. It will keep up your spirits and motivate you to keep going. Here's a suggestion from Katie, the improv expert, on how to do that. Make a sheet with the actions you're taking down the side and the days of the week across. Buy a package of inexpensive stickers. Then when you do what you said you would, give yourself a sticker. It will help you see your progress and keep your commitments to yourself.

with is to get interested in the "ready, fire, aim" process itself ("Now I'm getting feedback. How does that mean I need to revise my plan?") rather than the content of what's happening ("No, they didn't give me the job"/"My portfolio just went down again."). Making that mental switch will go a long way toward success in this phase.

Evaluate Progress

It requires a very unusual mind to undertake the analysis of the obvious. —ALFRED NORTH WHITEHEAD

Pamela Busch owns a restaurant in San Francisco. Like everyone else, she felt the pinch of the economic downturn as people stopped going out to eat. She decided to adapt by offering a three-course tasting menu at a set price. Her rationale? It helps diners to know exactly what they're going to spend in advance and is a bit of a bargain compared to buying the three courses separately. It's also, she says in an interview in the *San Francisco Chronicle,* "fiscally beneficial for restaurants because we know exactly what our food cost is going to run for each person . . . and that helps us gauge other aspects of our food budget."

Great. Her desired outcome is to stay in business. She's accepted the fact that change is needed, thought through her options, created a plan of action, and put her plan in place. What's next? Paying close attention to whether her plan is getting her the results she wants. Other restaurateurs are lowering prices, closing on Sundays and Mondays, switching to lower-end dining. Who's to say what or which combination will be effective? There are so many factors involved—where the restaurant is, the type of clientele, what happens with the economy, luck. . . . You can only know by trying.

Whatever change you're adjusting to, the evaluation phase is important, because you don't know what actions are actually going to get you where you want to go. You're taking your best guess, but if you don't stop to evaluate, you won't know if your guess paid off.

If you've just gotten a promotion, you're learning to drive results through other people, and you've started having weekly calls with your team to stay on top of what they're doing, you need a way of evaluating whether the weekly calls are working. Or if your boss got laid off, you've lost your air cover, and you go out looking for another powerful sponsor, you've got to stop and see what the person you've found is able to do for you. Or if you have to tighten your belt and you decide to make your own lunches and forgo the expensive coffee, great, but is it enough? You can't know if you don't run the numbers.

Here's an easy way to think about it. You know *what* you want—to stay in business, reduce debt, get a good mentor—but *how* you're going to make that happen is in the nature of an experiment. You try something, get a result, evaluate progress, and then readjust if necessary. You don't give up on the what unless you really have to, but your hows may change many times based on what you learn from your experiment.

I can't tell you how many times I observe people skipping the evaluation stage. They put something into action, assuming it will work, and never stop to analyze whether it actually is. Or they evaluate vaguely—sure, I'm saving money—but don't analyze exactly how much and whether it is making a significant enough difference. Or the situation continues to change but they don't look at it again because they put something in place and feel they're finished.

That's why part of your SMART action plan is careful evaluation. Measurements can be things like dollars in and out. Or results such as maintaining customers or the number of ideas your team comes up with and puts into action. Or feedback from others—"Yes, we see you making the changes you committed to." Don't get in the trap of analyzing time or effort spent; you can spend a lot of time on things that aren't getting you productive results. Challenge yourself to measure concrete results that matter.

Don't be tempted to skip this stage. When clients of mine take a new job, I always advise them to ask their boss

"NOT ALL ACTIONS ARE EQUAL"

"I'm a person who takes action because I can't stand the anxiety of the unknown," says Nancy, the owner of a remodeling firm. "It's resulted in my making a number of foolish choices. So I'm learning to get comfortable with not knowing and with using less force and more patience. That's helped me stay focused on making good choices and evaluating progress rather than impetuously taking action."

what results they are going to be evaluated on. Of course you have your own ideas of what's crucial, but you should at least know what the person who is going to evaluate you thinks. This is especially important when the job is amorphous or long range. Peter has just taken a job scouting for business opportunities in a country that is famous for complex deals that take years to materialize. How will he be evaluated next year? That's the question he's gone to his boss to find out.

Right now, stop and figure out what you're going to measure and when you will evaluate your progress. It's one of the ways to increase the likelihood of success.

If You're Not Stretching, You're Probably Missing Something

Life is like playing a violin in public and learning the instrument as one goes on. —SAMUEL BUTLER

"Can you send me over a draft of your book right away?" a friend asked when she heard what I was writing about. "I can't get my partners to learn this new online tool that has become crucial in our business. They keep doing it the way they've always done, but we can't afford that anymore. They've got to move with the times!"

I understand her partners' reluctance. I don't want to blog, learn how to do podcasts, network more, do online marketing, or get a camera for my computer so I can do Skype video conferencing. Yet these are all crucial marketing activities for a professional writer these days. I've written for thirty years without doing any of these things and I don't want to start now. My brain is perfectly happy doing what it's always done. After all, it does it so well!

Whoops, danger ahead. None of us, whatever our age, whatever our work, can afford that attitude anymore. The name of the game is staying relevant, and the life cycle of relevancy is getting shorter and shorter. It used to be that you got an education, then once you started working, while you may have gotten training now and then, the basics of your education held you in good stead for decades. Now, the world is so connected and the speed of change is so accelerated that we all need to be constantly learning new skills and tools. We can moan and complain about that fact, but if we want to maximize success, we need to accept that reality and get learning.

To do so we must get out of the safe zone and into the stretch zone. That's because learning means stretching yourself beyond your current limits. It means exerting more effort because it takes more work for the brain to do something new. It requires pushing your limits regarding what you can do and how you do it. The very fact that you feel awkward means you're learning—and that's a crucial thing!

To take this on in your own life means redefining *safe*, at least when it comes to work. Rather than seeing safety as a wonderful thing that we should strive for, we need to view it as a warning sign that we're coasting on past learning, rather than paying attention to what we need to take on next.

We all need to continually skill up. If you're not good at this, chances are you may not even know where to begin. So here are some tips:

- If you work with other people, ask them what new tools and techniques they're using and what trends in your field they're seeing—and then learn them yourself! If colleagues are asking you to use a new technology or you keep hearing about something new, consider it a favor that you've gotten the 411.

- If you work alone, go on the web and see what competitors are doing.

- If you're looking for work, as you network, ask people what industry trends they are seeing and what skills are required. Ask what's the first thing they'd learn if they were in your shoes.

- Track trends in your industry.

- If you need to get a whole new career going because yours has evaporated, check out those trend reports on recession-proof jobs. My brother in law is always threatening to go into health care for that very reason.

Here's a bonus to all this learning. Think of it as a gift from Nature for your hard work. It turns out that, just like our bodies, our brains need a good workout to stay healthy. And the workout must be one in which we're constantly learning new things to create new pathways so that as we age and pathways begin to disappear, we've got reserves. So if nothing else, think of it as making deposits into your brain's bank accounts for old age.

Like Samuel Butler says, we do have to learn as we live. When we really embrace the truth of that, we can learn to play beautiful music.

Do What's Needed

You don't get what you deserve. You get what you get.

—SYLVIA BOORSTEIN

Ryan had been a manager for a small company in New York's garment district. Then he got laid off and looked for work in his field for almost a year. Finally, he took advantage of the need for seasonal holiday workers and took a temporary job unloading pallets at night for Wal-Mart. "I'm so glad to have something productive to do," he explained, "and to be bringing money in, even if it's much less than I used to. I feel much better contributing to my family again."

Sometimes when change hits, we end up doing things we would rather not. With an Ivy League education, I've been a cashier in a drugstore, a mother's helper, and a housecleaner (all very temporarily, for which I am extremely grateful). I've worked the equivalent of three jobs for years and on more weekends than I care to remember. In tough times, my husband worked as a day laborer and sold books and other possessions on eBay, including a Wedgwood teapot that had been in his family for years. My fifty-two-year-old sister is an operating nurse who takes as many overnight calls as she can to bring in extra money for her family. There's a nurse in her OR who's still working in her seventies! Last night I heard Suze Orman suggest to a woman who was afraid her sixty-year-old husband was going to get laid off that he work harder than he ever has before to make himself indispensable to his company.

Some people have trouble with the need to get on with it with as much grace and grit as possible. I've been hearing a lot about couples who are struggling with this. One's gotten the memo that things must change; the other is dragging her heels. My guess is that it comes from a sense of entitlement. I worked for a while with a young woman fresh out of college who was continually outraged that she had to work as a receptionist because she "deserved" a more interesting job. This was a person whose parents were making up the difference between her income and her expenses, which ironically served to make her less grateful, not more, for her lot. It took all of my fortitude each week not to say, "At least you have a job." But I kept my mouth shut because such awareness never comes from the outside, only from experiences that teach us there's no such thing as "deserve."

Each and every person on the face of this earth "deserves" food and shelter and meaningful work. But unfortunately, as Buddhist teacher Sylvia Boorstein says in the opening quote, "You don't get what you deserve. You get what you get." That's why it's so important not to take whatever we have for granted. Every week at our PTP meeting, my colleague Andy Bryner expresses his thankfulness for having work at a time when so many don't. It's a valuable reminder.

Maya Angelou is a great role model of someone who did what was needed. Read her series of memoirs that begins with *I Know Why the Caged Bird Sings* if you're in need of inspiration. She learned from her grandmother never to complain. When she heard someone complaining, she'd say to Maya, "There are people all over the world, black and white, rich and poor, who went to sleep when that person went to sleep, and they have never awakened. . . . They would give anything for five minutes of what that person was complaining about." As a result, says Angelou, "I'll protest like the dickens, but I don't complain. . . . No matter how bad it gets, I'm always grateful to know that I don't have to stay with the negative."

Tough changes give us the opportunity to see just how tough we are. We roll up our sleeves and do what's needed. (Within the bounds of what's legal and moral, I hope.) We

REDEFINE *LOWLY*

"I remember years ago, when I was at a big agency," says Tina, a successful talent agent. "I'd been promoted from second assistant to first assistant/junior agent. I still worked directly under and for the head of the department, but I no longer had to do the bottom-tier assistant stuff. My boss was pretty demanding, but I'd managed to survive two years literally fetching coffee, taking dictation, catering to his every need, and now I felt free, really accomplished. At one point the person he'd hired as his second assistant quit, and while he was interviewing for a new one, he required that I step back into that role. I was pretty snotty about it—felt demeaned, humiliated to have to take a step back, embarrassed to be seen carrying coffee again, etc. I let him know that both verbally and in my behavior. One day he pulled me into his office, shut the door, and said, 'Part of being successful is knowing the difference between being persecuted and being a team player. I'm not punishing you by making you do these things; I'm asking you to fill a need until someone else takes the job.' This lesson has helped me stay flexible throughout my career. When I have to do something for someone in my business life that might otherwise seem 'lowly,' I remember that I'm actually *choosing* to do it for the greater success of all of us."

experience how work, even unloading pallets, makes us feel good. And the dignity that comes from the determination to do what's necessary, that "starch in the backbone," as Maya Angelou calls it, can never be taken from us.

Build Your Brand

Discover your brand by pinpointing your unique service and identity. —DR. JASON A. DEITCH

Jason A. Deitch is a doctor and author who teaches other doctors "that today's new health care economy requires us to adapt in order to survive." He has five secrets. One is "create your brand." Jason thinks that when it comes to this, "doctors might just be the absolute worst marketers . . . on the entire planet."

Well, Jason, I'm not so sure. I spend a lot of my time helping clients from all walks of life understand the need for branding and then strategizing how to do it. I'll never forget the corporate client who said to me, "I thought that if I did a great job, people would know and I'd get promoted." "Doing a great job is only part of your job," I replied. "The other is making sure other people know who you are, because otherwise they are too focused on themselves to pay attention to you."

Business buzz words come and go. I tend to ignore them. But the idea that we must all create a brand and market ourselves is one that has not just staying power but that has gained in importance as the world is changing. Brand is

all about reputation—what you're known for. It is made up
of what you do well, your talents, and what people can expect from you. As Jason Deitch says, it communicates "who
you are, what you offer, and most importantly, how people
will benefit from working with you."

No matter what position you are in—entrepreneur,
small-business owner, corporate vice president—and what
job you have or want to have, you need to clearly understand your brand and then make it known to others. Terry
Wood, the CBS executive responsible for launching
Rachael Ray's and Dr. Phil's shows, said in a recent interview that one of the things that characterizes successful
folks is that they know the answer to two questions: "What
do I want to be known for? What makes me different? . . . Famous can be overrated, but if I'm known for
something, and that defines who I am, I can take it to the
bank." That's what brand is.

What do you want to be known for? What makes you
different? I think of it as your unique form of greatness. Go
back to the four elements of LIVE (what you love, inner
gifts, values, and environments that bring out the best in
you) that you identified in previous chapters and condense
them into a sentence. Here's an example: "I'm great at taking ideas that others come up with and turning them into
saleable products in a tight time frame by myself." Now
think about the benefits to others of your brand: "You
don't have to supervise me, and I'm good at anticipating
what could go wrong so you save time and money."

Now, think about who needs to know about you and
your brand. Your customers? Your boss? "But I don't want

to be seen as bragging," you're probably thinking. This is not bragging. It's a simple statement of what you uniquely have to offer. The more you embrace who you are and what you're good at, the more you can communicate it in such a way that it comes off as an accurate statement of the truth, with you being appropriately confident. And the more you focus on the benefits for the person on the other side, the more they'll be so captivated by them that they'll only be grateful that you can offer such a wonderful thing!

Next you have to decide how you're going to let people know. You can look for opportunities to bring it up, or use it as an elevator speech when searching for a job. Or if you have your own business, like a doctor, you could create a flyer for your office. When you do something great, make sure you let the appropriate people know. Look for ways to quantify it. I have a client who simply sends out a one-line analysis once a month to her boss and her boss's boss, quantifying the results her marketing efforts have achieved in dollars. When I talk about my work as a thinking partner, I let prospective clients know that when I worked with a group of women at Microsoft, 80 percent of them got a raise and/or promotion within six months. That gets people's attention and differentiates me from others out there.

Brand isn't communicated solely through words. It's something you create from all of your actions—from the way you answer e-mails to coming up with a great idea at a meeting. Bottom line: you want the people who matter to say the same thing about you that you say in your brand statement, for example, "Boy, is he great at coming up with ideas that sell and getting to the right people!"

"IT CAN'T HURT"

"I wanted to go to art school but didn't have all the right requirements," said John. "I decided to try by visiting the school and talking to a professor on the admissions committee to hopefully market myself with him. He encouraged me to apply and submit my portfolio. After the visit I sent a thank-you saying, based on your suggestions I will go ahead and apply. He then wrote back offering to look at my portfolio and make suggestions as to what to include. I did that, then sent a thank-you for his suggestions, which I took. Then I asked what I could be doing to prepare while I was waiting to find out if I got in, what websites, etc. would he recommend for me to learn more about graphic design. I figured he'd think of me as someone who was very eager, open to feedback, and willing to work hard. Lots of people think, 'Why bother?' when it comes to thank-yous, etc. I think, 'What does it hurt to try and make a good impression, to let him know the kind of person I am?' And yes, I did get in."

Putting an effort into branding and communicating your brand will give you a competitive advantage during change, whether you are looking for work, looking for advancement, looking for networks, or looking for customers or clients.

Get More Connected

Call it a clan, call it a network, call it a tribe, call it a family.
Whatever you call it, whoever you are, you need one.

—JANE HOWARD

My friend Kathleen is an elementary school principal in California, which is rated forty-seventh out of fifty states in funding per student. I've known her for fifteen years and have watched her gracefully ride all kinds of change waves in public education. When I asked her how she's managed to adapt so well, she immediately started talking about her networks.

"Well," she said, "I regularly call a dinner meeting with other principals in the district. I call it the prin din. We talk over ideas, brainstorm responses to things coming from above, offer resources to one another. And I rely heavily on my parent council at school to provide guidance to me in areas that I don't know as much about. For instance, one dad who's in finance looked at where our emergency fund was and had me break it up into smaller pieces at various banks to keep it safer. And that was before the banks started crashing! I've created a network of support staff at school, those of us there's only one of—the librarian, the janitor, the secretary, and me. We regularly meet to deal with the issues we have in common. They see things I don't. Finally, I've created a network of learning for and with my teachers by corralling people I know in the private sector, like you, to do leadership development, and invite guest speakers in educational theory, etc., so we can keep up."

I've always thought of *network* as a dirty word, as it seemed to involve talking to random strangers at cocktail parties. Those things never did a thing for me. But Kathleen helped me see that we are all embedded in various networks already and that when we're going through a change, tapping those networks—for guidance, for ideas on what you need to be learning, for their take on coming trends, among many other things—is crucial.

Nowhere is this more important than when looking for work. I personally don't know one person who's gotten a job through online job sites, despite having posted sometimes hundreds of résumés out there. Everyone has gotten work through their network—either directly or through a six-degrees-of-separation thing. And you never know which network or connection will be the one. My older daughter got a great job from being introduced to a person in the company by a volleyball teammate. And networks are not just for jobs. They can help you find an inexpensive place to live, a date, a great doctor when you need it. . . .

Even if you think of yourself as a terrible networker, you have networks. Take me, for instance. I think of myself as a lone wolf. But if I really think about it, I have several networks—a network of friends, a network of PTP trainers, a network of parents at my daughter's school, a network of parents with kids adopted from China, a network of people in publishing, a network of clients, a network of fans of my books. How about you? What are your networks, and what sort of skills and resources do the people in them represent? Write them down so you can see them. Hopefully, the list itself will give you some comfort.

Now that you've got an idea of your connections, what

TIPS FOR JOB NETWORKING

Diane Darling is the CEO of Effective Networks and an author on the subject. Here are some of her tips for networking if you're looking for a job:

- Learn about the person you're reaching out to. "In the old days it was gossip. Now it's Google."

- Control what others find out about you when they Google you. Buy your name as a domain name (it only costs $10 a year) and put up a simple one-page website. Think of it as a marketing tool that you'll have your whole life. You can do it yourself or get one for very little money.

- Join LinkedIn and Facebook.

- Get comfortable with the role of a job seeker—practice what you are going to say. Make an A, B, and C list of people to talk to—A being the ones you really think can help. Start with the Cs so by the time you get to the As you are completely comfortable.

- Get a networking buddy, a person who is looking for something in the same field—say, publishing—but a different department, such as finance and marketing. It not only makes it easier to go to networking events if you have someone with you, but you can trade connections.

is it that you want help with? Is it a job resource? Help in avoiding foreclosure? A good therapist? When you reach out, remember that networking goes two ways; be sure to ask, "Is there some way I can I help you?" Think about who you could connect them to. The more you think of networking as building a web of relationships, the easier it is to do. And don't forget to thank the person for the information and contacts.

If it's work you're looking for, it's best not to ask directly for a job. Instead, ask for help; Do you know anyone I can talk to? What's your perspective on the industry? What trends are you seeing? What should I be learning now? I'm looking in these areas, what other areas would you suggest given my experience and talents? Who else should I talk to? Make sure you leave with a lead to at least one other person and have it be as warm a hand-off as possible. The best is if the person makes the connection for you via an e-mail or phone intro. You're more likely to get traction. At minimum, ask if you can use their name.

When you're connected to a new person, be persistent but not a pest. They won't always respond, even if someone they know has made the connection. Don't take it personally. If you do get to speak to them, come prepared with things to offer that he or she might find useful. Every discussion and interaction builds your brand. And remember, you never know which connection can lead you to what you want.

Don't just network in a time of need. We all need to stay connected to others as much as possible so we have communities of support to rely on. Networking provides visibility and connections. Your network is a web of folks you can count on, advocates for you out there in the world. Think of networking when you don't "need" to as an investment in the future. Relationships are things you must keep going, or they die on the vine. See how and where you can expand your connections.

Reach out. We need one another in times like this.

_____

Create a Change Masters Circle

When the world seems to be falling apart, . . . hang onto your own ideals and find kindred spirits. That's the rule of life.   —JOSEPH CAMPBELL

Just before he died at age ninety-six, Studs Terkel, who'd written an oral history of the Great Depression, among many other books, was asked what he'd learned about that time that he could offer as advice for getting through the sea changes we're experiencing now. His reply? "Don't blame yourself. Turn to others. Take part in the community. The big boys are not that bright."

One of the possible great outcomes of learning to adapt to the changes we're facing right now is that it will help us turn more toward one another. There's a particular strength that we can find in the company of others, as those who've been part of a 12-step program know very well.

In his book *Change or Die,* Alan Deutschman studied people who've made huge, lasting changes—such as heart attack patients and drug addicts who permanently changed their lifestyles for the better. Although the odds for lasting success aren't so good—about one in ten—one factor the successful 10 percent had in common was, according to Deutschman, "a new, emotional relationship with a . . . community that inspires and sustains hope." This community also "helps you learn, practice and master the new habits and skills that you'll need," he writes.

A community can also pool resources, as a colleague of mine recently reminded me. She was telling me about a friend who'd decided to have a garage "sale" in which she gave away the things she no longer needed. It was so popular that now her garage is the site of a neighborhood weekly giveaway, where people who have stuff they no longer want or need put it out for others who need it to take.

Perhaps you already have a community of support through your church or neighborhood. Or you have formed a monthly circle with like-minded folks, as friends of mine have been doing for decades. If not, allow me to suggest that you create one. I got an e-mail the other day that gave me an idea. One of my readers wrote, "I have been a psychologist for over twelve years and was thrilled to find your book *This Year I Will. . . .* It was the perfect book at the perfect time. I felt that my friends and I (all struggling through our marriages) would benefit from a group based around your book. My friends and I will be getting together every two weeks to review chapters, check in on successes and failures at keeping our goals, etc."

Sounds great to me! How about if you created a Change Masters circle with folks you know? You could meet regularly to discuss what you're working on and be a resource for one another. There are all kinds of things you can do.

Recently I was on a call with a circle of PTP trainers and we discussed the kinds of things a group could do to support one another through change. Here is some of what the dozen or so of us came up with. Some ideas rely on left-brained, analytic thinking and some on right-brained symbolic and imagistic thinking because we need to engage both halves of our brain when we face challenges:

- Bring a symbol of something you trust in yourself and share it with one other person, and then talk to one another about this question, what do you need to trust yourself more deeply in the situation you're in?

- Tell a story to a partner about a hard time you went through, with the listener listening for the inner resources you used to get through it. Switch. Then have the pairs share each other's stories with the whole. By having the story told and retold, the insights become engrained.

- Create a list of creative ideas for getting through hard times.

- Have a resource sharing time—let one another know the kinds of skills, talents, and connections each of you has to offer. It will help not only the person receiving help but also the giver, who gets a gift—the gift of self-respect that he has something of value to offer.

- Introduce the four Domains of Competence (See "What Are Your Inner Talents"). Think about which domain you almost never use. That's where we tend to worry. Then find a person in the group who's strong in that way of thinking to brainstorm ideas with, to receive guidance and support.

- Invite older people who've been through tough economic times before to offer their wisdom.

· Go to www.imaginechicago.org and find out what this group did to revitalize their community. It's a movement that's spread all over the world.

It doesn't have to even be a face-to-face community. Online communities can be tremendously helpful because there is more anonymity. You don't have to admit your situation to people you know, but can easily connect to others in the same boat, even across long distances.

There's a Hassidic saying that beautifully captures the essence of what community can offer us: "When a man is singing and cannot lift his voice, and another comes and sings with him, one who can lift his voice, the first will be able to lift his voice, too. That is the secret of the bond between spirits." We need to strengthen those bonds now.

Use an Inspiring Mantra to Keep Up Your Spirits

Every tomorrow has two handles. You can take hold of the handle of anxiety or the handle of enthusiasm. Upon our choice so will be the day. —ANONYMOUS

When I was a child, dealing with my particular configuration of a dysfunctional family, I remember lying awake in bed night after night, year after year, too afraid to go to sleep. There were some willow trees outside my window I used to watch. No matter how hard the wind blew, and how far the trees bent, they never broke. I took on that image as my personal courage mantra. For years, whenever things happened that upset me, I would say to myself, "I'm like the willow. I can bend but I won't break."

I don't know where I got the idea—certainly no one taught me. But I truly believe that that saying saved my life. It reminded me of my resilience whenever I needed it. And of the fact that I'd survived thus far and therefore was likely to continue to do so. I felt it as an exhortation, as a surge of determination to get through my childhood as intact as possible. It allowed me to embrace the challenges with as much enthusiasm as I possibly could. I'd be damned if I were going to break and I would prove it to the world that I could survive!

The power of that image was so significant to me that I've hesitated to call it a mantra, because I didn't want to sound too New Agey. But then I read an article by spiritual teacher Eknath Easwaran calling a mantra a spiritual formula that "has the capacity to transform consciousness" because it calls "up what is best and deepest in ourselves." It's as close an explanation for what it did for me as I can come up with. So I want it to work its power, whatever that may be, on you, too. We all have negative mantras we say to ourselves constantly: "I can't handle this, this is too much, I'll never survive it. . . ." You know your particular version. So why not have an uplifting one to counteract it?

My mantra was so helpful that if I could only offer you

one thing from all the ideas in this book, it would be for you to find an image, phrase, or metaphor that sustains you as you ride the waves of change. It doesn't have to be something you say. One former client has a keychain with a tiny woman surfer on it to remind herself that she can stay up on the board. Your mantra just needs to be something that encourages your heart and strengthens your spirit as you navigate in the unknown.

Focus on the Upside of Scaling Back

> Manifest plainness,
> Embrace simplicity,
> Reduce selfishness,
> Have few desires.
>
> —LAO-TZU

Some years ago, I was having money troubles and needed to sell my house and move to somewhere smaller. My mother was horrified. "What will your friends and neighbors think?" she cried. "That I had to downsize," I replied.

Unwanted change often brings embarrassment about our need to scale back. We don't want others to know that we have huge credit-card debt or lost a job or that our business went belly-up. We want to feel—and appear—competent to run our own lives successfully. And the fact that we have to get our clothes at Goodwill, for instance, may feel like some kind of a failure that we need to hide from others, but when we focus on what others may think of us, we run the danger of losing touch with the good choices we need to make in order to adapt. So how can we avoid worrying about what other people think?

One of the advantages of what's happening right now is that it's happening to everyone. Virtually no one is immune. Whether you're coping with having to lay off the gardener or what to do with your kids in the summer because you can't afford to send them to camp but need to work, or having to declare bankruptcy, you're not alone. What will the neighbors think? They're too busy thinking about their own need to scale back to give yours much attention, unless it's to wish they had your worries. Remembering we're all in a similar boat can be helpful.

The other best thing we can do is focus on the upside of the adapting we're doing. Psychologists call this reframing. I have a friend who has an absolutely gorgeous cottage that she has decorated completely from castoffs she's found in the street, items from Goodwill, and other unlikely places. The story she tells herself is not, "I'm so poor I have to find things on the street," but "I love to find discarded treasures and fix them up. I love to create a beautiful space from virtually nothing." The second story focuses on the upside of what she's doing and allows her to hold her head up high.

Here's another example. A client of mine is a self-confessed impulsive shopper. She named that part of herself Suzy Shop. I asked her recently what Suzy Shop was doing now that there was no money to run to the mall. "She's having a great time finding ways to save as much money as possible" was the reply.

Get how it works? What could be right about the scaling back you're doing right now? How can you reframe it as something advantageous? "I turned our fancy car back in and got something cheaper," a friend who owns a shoe store told me the other day. "That's a savings of five hundred a month, which translates into ten fewer pairs of shoes I have to sell and a lot more peace of mind." The more you focus on the upside, the better you'll feel and the less you'll care about what others think of your choices.

Here's some research to inspire your reframing. Psychology professor Tim Kasser, author of *The High Price of Materialism*, did a study that compared two hundred voluntary simplifers (folks who've chosen to live simply) with average folks. He found that even though the simplifiers made an average of $15,000 less than the other group, they were "significantly happier." In fact, he found, the things we think we want—money, stuff, status—can lead to dissatisfaction, even depression. "People who pursue intrinsic values—self-acceptance, making the world a better place, helping polar bears—are much happier," he explains. "If you orient your life around personal growth and family and community, you'll feel better." So chances are the changes you're making can lead to greater happiness, not less.

Once you've reframed your downsizing for yourself, talk to others about the positive changes you're making. Shame grows in the dark of silence. Once you bring your adjustments out into the open in the new frame, you'll likely feel much better. As the wise woman Maya Angelou said, you can be changed by circumstances, but you don't have to be reduced by them.

"IT'S BECOME A FUN THING WE DO TOGETHER"

"When Chloe was a baby and toddler, I was really, really into buying her clothes," Jill explained. "I loved dressing her up in fancy outfits. It was something I took a lot of joy in, since dressing myself is a big means of creative expression for me. Obviously, clothes like that cost a bit of money. When I had to start paying close attention to my budget, I looked at what I was spending on her clothes and quickly saw it couldn't continue. So I learned my way around eBay fast. Now I spend literally about a fifth the price on Chloe's clothes. I feel empowered, and I also feel really good about teaching her to recycle items we don't need anymore. She and I look at things together online, she tells me which ones she likes, and then she cheers for me: 'Go mama, go— win that hat!' She gets so excited when we win an auction. It's become a fun thing that we do together."

Allow Your Circumstances to Open Your Heart

What is to give light must endure burning.

—VIKTOR FRANKL

I was giving a workshop in Oman on conflict resolution. My host informed me that the CEO of one of the largest businesses in the country would attend and had asked to take me out to lunch afterward. Gratefully, I said yes. And that's how I met Mohammed, one of the warmest CEOs I've ever encountered. He was there because he cared deeply about developing his employees and wanted to learn about PTP's work.

At lunch, his story came out. His extended family owned businesses across the Middle East. He and his wife were born and lived their early lives in Kuwait. In 1990, when Iraq invaded Kuwait, he and his family had to flee to Saudi Arabia in their car, leaving everything behind. Their businesses and home were destroyed. "When we crossed the border," he said, with sadness in his eyes, "there were people standing by the side of the road handing out water bottles. I realized that I had been rich, but I was now in need of that water as much as every other refugee on the road."

Mohammed came to Oman and rebuilt his life. But, I realized, he hadn't forgotten that day when he was in need. He allowed his experience to open his heart and grow his compassion. He knew what it was like to be in need and used that awareness to be kind to those he encountered in business, whether employee, customer, or vendor. "I never imagined becoming CEO," he told me modestly, but I wasn't surprised that he had.

Unasked-for change is a great leveler, as Mohammed found out. Suddenly we're aware that we're part of a huge human community struggling for survival. Then we're faced with a choice. We can see it as every person for him- or herself and try to grab whatever goodies are available. Or we can allow our awareness that we're all in this together to open our hearts and offer as much kindness and help as we can.

There is a practice in Buddhism that helps take what you're dealing with and use it to grow compassion. Here's how to do it. Bring to mind the things you are struggling with and recognize that millions of other people are in the same boat: "Just as I am having trouble adapting, so are people everywhere; just like I am scared, so are people everywhere; just as I want security, so do people everywhere." Whatever phrases come to your mind are the right ones. It helps you feel less alone and hopefully more connected to the rest of the human community.

I'm writing this at Thanksgiving, when the news is full of stories about how donations at food banks are down but volunteerism is up. Maybe we're all getting it. Maybe one of the effects of this monster wave of change we're all trying to cope with is that we'll turn toward one another, not against. I fervently hope so.

STEP 4: STRENGTHEN ADAPTABILITY

We live in a moment of history where change is so speeded
up that we begin to see the present only when it is already
disappearing.   —R. D. LAING

Congratulations! If you've come this far, you've done a lot
of work in accepting the reality of your situation, expanding your thinking about possibilities, and taking appropriate and timely action. The benefit of consciously going
through the cycle is that, having gone through it once,
you've earned your stripes as a Change Master. You'll be
better prepared for the next time life calls on you to adapt.
And it will—have no doubt. This is an ongoing journey as
we engage with the fast-moving times we live in.

That's why it's so vital that you stop and notice what you
did. Learning is strengthened when we take time to reflect
on what we've learned—you wouldn't want to waste any of
your hard-won lessons, would you? This final stage is more
than a resting spot, however. There are things you can do to
keep in shape AdaptAbility-wise so that when the next wave
hits, it will feel more like a splash in a placid pool.

Become a Lifelong Learner

> We now accept the fact that learning is a lifelong process of
> keeping abreast of change. And the most pressing task is to
> teach people how to learn.   —PETER DRUCKER

My mother has been telling me she's too old to change since she was forty-five; she's now eighty-five. In a way, she had the privilege of that position because she hasn't had to support herself. Those of us out there making a living know how much the world is changing and how we must change to keep up, no matter what our age. I just read somewhere that the average American will have nine jobs by the time she is thirty-two. How many therefore by the time she's sixty-two?

In his book *Innovation and Entrepreneurship,* management consultant Peter F. Drucker claims that we're moving into an entrepreneurial society in which people must continue to learn new things their entire lifetimes and must "take responsibility for their learning, their own self-development, and their own careers."

What kinds of skills and education will you and I need? Since we don't even know what will happen tomorrow, how can we possibly prepare for two decades from now? Or four? We can't. That's why one key component of being a Change Master is to become a lifelong learner, which will give us greater capacity to cope with whatever comes our way. According to Stanford psychology professor Carole Dweck, here are the key attitudes:

- belief that you can learn
- trust that your efforts to learn will pay off
- willingness to persist
- seeing mistakes and feedback as learning opportunities
- finding inspiration from the success of others

I find some of these easier than others. I've got no trouble with the first three or the last one. I'm still working on seeing mistakes as learning opportunities. There continues to be a voice of perfectionism inside me that panics when I find I've made an error, although the voice is much softer than it used to be. And I still have trouble seeking out feedback because I'm afraid it will be negative. But I'm working on it! I've gotten much better at feeling the discomfort and asking for input anyway.

Looking at the list, how are you doing on becoming a lifelong learner? Which of these are easy? Difficult? Try to

KEEP ON DOING NEW THINGS

Challenge yourself in times of less stress to keep learning by taking on new things. It doesn't have to be something huge. Read different kinds of books, see different kinds of movies, talk to new people, expose yourself to new experiences, learn new skills. Put changes of your choosing into action. The more comfortable you get with change, the more agile you'll be.

notice without beating yourself up. That just interferes with a learning attitude because it reinforces the belief that you should know everything already.

The capacity to learn is truly our greatest asset in the unknown because no matter what the future holds in store for us, we're holding the key to successful adaptation. We can't know now all of what we will need to know because we don't know what that is yet. But we can trust that we'll be able to learn it when we need to.

Reflect on Your Learnings

No prairie fire can burn the grass up
when spring breezes blow, it will again sprout.
—ANCIENT CHINESE POEM QUOTED IN HA JIN'S *A FREE LIFE*

About a year after my painful divorce, I was sitting on an Oakland hillside where thousands of houses and trees had burned to the ground just about the same time as my marriage had broken up. As I surveyed the devastation, I realized that my life felt like it had been razed just like the hillside. I could see tiny green shoots reaching up out of the blackened earth and I knew I had shoots of new life sprouting in me as well.

Change *can* knock us flat, but it always gives us opportunities to grow, even if it's hard to see while we're going through it. That's why it's so important after the fact to take a step back and see how we've developed as a result of what we've gone through. That way, our newfound resources are more available to us in the future.

When I think of people I know who are Change Masters, one of the first who comes to mind is Mary Beth Sammons, author of seven books, including *We Carry Each Other: Getting Through Life's Toughest Times.* I've known her eight years. During that time, her father died after a long illness and she was his primary caretaker; her son had a life-threatening car crash and, later, a serious illness; she went through a difficult divorce; her best friend and neighbor dropped dead; and several other close friends died. And, oh yes, she got laid off—five times.

"It's been interesting," she said when I called her to ask what she's learned through all this change. "I've alternated between doing freelance marketing, PR, and writing, and doing those things within organizations. Every time I go in-house because I want security, the tier I'm in gets wiped out shortly after. What have I learned? First of all, to really not take it personally and to move on quickly. One of my jobs folded on my birthday, just as I was celebrating my newfound stability. That wiped me out for weeks. Now I just get up the next day and think, "That's done, what's the next opportunity?"

"Instead of trying to grasp something similar, I've gotten good at taking each experience I've had and creating something new out of it. Recently I've gotten a lot of assignments about reinventing your life and being in the sandwich generation, about how to give care while keeping up your career. Things I was forced to learn because of the situation I was in. I observe a need and match my expertise to it.

"I've stopped listening to what everybody else says you should do. I have much more of an entrepreneurial spirit than I had before. I used to go to organizations and say, 'Here's what you should be doing. I'll create it for you.' Now I think, "I'll create it for myself and sell it to them."

"I've learned to honor my grieving as each change hits—sadness, anger, fear. And I think everyone needs some kind of spiritual practice to sustain them. My faith has really helped me keep going.

"Finally, I've learned to do something life-giving for myself no matter what else is going on. Once when a job ended and I was feeling bad about myself, I decided that I was going to train for and compete in a triathlon. And I did! I'd always been a couch potato so it was a very big deal to accomplish this thing I never thought I could do in my life. It gave me confidence that in work, I could take on something new and succeed."

Do you see some themes in Mary Beth's story that also weave throughout this book? That's because hers are the actions of a person who's good at AdaptAbility. Like most of us, Mary Beth learned these lessons along the way, as she faced each wave and adapted as best she could. They often came with a lot of pain and struggle. I'm hoping that as a result of reading her story as well as the rest of this book, you can now adapt with greater ease.

Like Mary Beth, you've gone through changes and made it to this point. So I want you to take some time right now and reflect on what you've learned so far about change agility. To perhaps journal or take a few notes. Because even though we swear we will never forget the lessons of this experience, we do. Having a written record ensures you don't lose the wisdom you've gained. Keep it where you can pull it out when you need it.

Here are some reflection questions to get you started:

- What worked and why?

- What didn't work and why? The *why* is important because it may have to do with the circumstances rather
  than the idea itself. It might be a great strategy at another time.

- What would you improve upon in yourself next time
  you face change?

- What inner resources did you use from the past?
  What new ones did you cultivate?

- What tools and techniques helped you be positive
  and focused?

- Who were your best allies?

- What qualities of heart, mind, and spirit do you
  have now that you didn't have before or have you
  made stronger in yourself? How can you offer those
  to others?

- What can you do in an ongoing way to stay in touch
  with your LIVE elements so they remain a strong
  foundation?

When you look for the green shoots in the blackened hillside, you recognize how you've grown. You've cultivated
competencies and skills you never had before, as well as
beautiful soul qualities like greater patience, gratitude, and
acceptance. Most likely you've actually grown new path-

ways and cells in your brain and strengthened your mind's capacity to cope with adversity. You're stronger and wiser, with greater trust in your capacity to face whatever changes come your way.

That's the amazing thing about the changes we didn't ask for. We do all we can to avoid them, but when forced to adapt, we encounter our greatest opportunities for growth and development. As a Native American saying goes, "The soul would have no rainbows if the eyes had no tears."

Through being tumbled around on the rocks of change, we are polished to our greatest brilliance. The journey isn't complete and our efforts are not fully redeemed until we offer that brilliance back. The world needs what only you have to give based on all that you are and all that you have learned through this journey of change. I wonder, where and how will you shine?

IV.
Twenty Quick Tips for Surviving Change You Didn't Ask For

1. Focus on the solution, not the problem. Because society rewards analytic thinking, we believe that identifying the cause of our troubles is the answer: Why is this happening? That's a starting point, but don't spend too much time there. What are you going to do about where you are?

2. Because feeling in control is so crucial to resilience, and unasked-for-change can leave us feeling very out of control, try asking yourself this question during the day: What am I free to choose right now?

3. What if you don't believe you have the confidence or talent to find a solution? Pretend you do. Turns out that "fake it till you make it" has validity in brain science—the thoughts you hold and actions you take really do create new pathways in your brain. "As we act, so we become," as Sharon Begley puts it in *Train Your Mind, Change Your Brain.*

4. Find things to laugh about. People who thrive during change work their funny bones. Says psychologist Mihaly Csikszentmihalyi, "Thrivers' happiness is not dependent on external factors or life circumstances

alone. It derives from their chosen state of consciousness and ability to cheer themselves up when things are looking down." Laughter has been shown to relieve stress, lower blood pressure, and improve breathing as well as mood. Best of all is when we can laugh at ourselves for not being perfect or when we hit some roadblock in the direction we wanted to go. It helps us stay lighthearted and resourceful.

5. Celebrate success along the way, no matter how small: a new connection, a possible lead, a small savings. Give yourself credit for moving forward in a difficult situation. At the end of the day, look at what you've done and celebrate whatever accomplishment you can. Celebration creates positive energy and forward momentum.

6. When considering options, before you say something won't work, consider how it might work. Try it on for a while.

7. Focus on a positive future. Ricki Lake put it this way: "When I went through challenges in my life . . . I told myself, 'Focus on where you'll be a year from now.' It helps to know that, in time, the hard parts will be water under the bridge." I'd modify that to, focus on where you *want* to be a year from now (otherwise you can scare yourself with all kinds of terrible futures). Then ask what actions you need to take today to make that positive future happen.

8. Breathe slowly and deeply. Shallow breathing is a sign that you are in fight-or-flight mode, where you

are not in touch with all of your resources to handle this change. A few conscious slow and deep breaths, especially if you also relax your muscles as much as possible, tells the part of your brain responsible for fight or flight that you're not in danger and so it calms down. Then you're able to think more clearly, widely, and deeply. To test if you're breathing deeply, put one hand on your chest, the other on your belly. Take a breath in and one out. Are both hands moving? If only the top one is, see if you can get the bottom one going as well.

9. Direct your complaints upward. Sometimes all we can do when faced with a challenging change is to cry out to the heavens, "Help me!" That's what AA is all about—turning your problem over to a Higher Power, however you understand that to be, so that you aren't so alone in the difficulty. Writes Carol Orsborn in her book *The Art of Resilience,* "You don't have to believe that this works for it to be effective." Give it a try.

10. Get out and help someone else. As Studs Terkel put it in one of his last interviews, "Once you become active helping others, you feel alive. You don't feel, 'it's my fault.' You become a different person. And others are changed too.' When we focus on someone else's problems, we put our own in perspective. Plus we take a break from worrying about ourselves, which is always a good thing. A friend who was in a California fire zone last summer e-mailed me during the time it wasn't clear whether she lost her house,

saying, "If we focus on helping others, panic diminishes." Absolutely!

11. Find someone in the same situation to help and pay attention to what you suggest they do. One of your best resources is the advice you give others. Be sure to follow your own suggestions.

12. With apologies to those of us who shun it, thirty minutes of aerobic activity daily is still the best way, experts say, to counteract the stress of change.

13. Encourage yourself along the way as you would a child running a race—"You can do it! You're doing well!" This positive self-talk has been found to increase what psychologists call agency—the belief you can get where you want to go.

14. If you find yourself worrying all the time, set aside a fifteen-minute worry time, say 5 p.m. every day. Then when your mind starts worrying at other times, tell yourself it's not worry time and distract yourself—read a good book, do a puzzle, something that occupies your mind.

15. If you find yourself having to do things you'd rather not, make sure that you also do things you love on a regular basis: my friend Annette traces her family tree 'cause she loves genealogy, Andy plays the piano, I read novels. Passionate interests give zest to life during change. They don't have to be expensive.

16. Be sure to thank those who help along the way. Gratefulness is good for your mind, body, and spirit

and it increases the possibility that you will continue to receive assistance.

17. What really matters here? That's a question that will help you keep the change in proportion. A woman who lost her house was told by her minister that what she needed was a home, not a house. It helped her move to a rental with greater peace and perspective.

18. Hang out with happy people. A large new twenty-year study by Harvard medical sociologist Nicholas Christakis shows that happiness is contagious, spreading from one person to nearby family members, neighbors, and friends. One happy person can increase the happiness of others he or she comes into contact with by 8 to 36 percent and the effect can last up to a year. Ride on the uplift of others. It will give you the energy to keep on.

19. Quakers are taught to look for "way open" to know if they should pursue something and "way closed" to give up. That means they look for the open door to indicate which way to go and if they encounter too many obstacles, they conclude it wasn't meant to be. That's a good strategy for all of us coping with change. Yes, you should be focused on what you want, but if all pathways to a goal are blocked, perhaps that's a message to give up and pursue something else entirely. As Anthony D'Angelo says, "Never let your persistence and passion turn into stubbornness and ignorance."

20. Focus on the positive qualities you have to face this change. I recently got my town newsletter and in it, an administrator named Audrey Lee wrote, "The year ahead may be lean in fiscal resources, but I know we are rich in energy, talent, commitment and momentum." I instantly knew the town was in good hands. The more we pay attention to the resources we have to cope, the better we will do, particularly when we ask ourselves how we can use our energy, talent, commitment, and momentum to succeed.

V.
Resources for More Support

CAREER

http://10goodminutes.com: a series of ten-minute podcasts on things from networking to interviewing. It promotes itself to young professionals, but there's good stuff here for all ages.

The Occupational Information Network site (www .careerdevelopment-resources.net) is also a good one, giving information on career requirements of more than 950 job titles, as well as resources for development, training, résumé writing, etc. You can even search for occupations that use your existing skills.

CREATIVITY

The Open Mind by Dawna Markova (Conari Press, 1996) can help identify how your mind processes information and how to access your most creative thinking.

Caffeine for the Creative Mind by Stefan Mumaw and Wendy Lee Oldfield (How, 2006) offers hundreds of exercises to jump-start creative thinking.

DEBT AND OTHER MONEY ISSUES

www.smartcookies.com: five women from Vancouver started a get-out-of-debt club that has expanded to a website, radio and TV shows, and a column. On their website, you can join a money group to help you set goals and stay on track as well as read all kinds of money-saving tips.

All of Suze Orman's stuff is great—books, TV show, online resources. Go to suzeorman.com to see what's available. Her Action Plans are particularly useful.

Some credit-card companies are offering alerts to remind you when your payment is due so you don't pay a late fee, or to let you know when you're getting close to your limit. See if yours does.

DIVORCE

The best book I know about surviving a breakup is *Coming Apart: Why Relationships End and How to Live Through the Ending of Yours* by Daphne Rose Kingma (Conari Press, 2000).

DOWNSIZING

Your Money or Your Life: 9 Steps for Transforming Your Relationship with Money and Achieving Financial Success by Vicki Robins and Joe Dominguez (Penguin, revised, 2008) can help you reset priorities and live better with less.

Secrets of Simplicity: Learn to Live Better With Less (Chronicle Books, 2008) by Mary Carlomagno offers a step-by-step process for decluttering your home.

The PBS series *Simple Living with Wanda Urbanska:* check your local listing to see if and when it's broadcast in your area.

EMOTIONS

Emotional Alchemy: How the Mind Can Heal the Heart by Tara Bennett-Goleman (Three Rivers Press, 2002) not only explains why our habitual fears get triggered under stress, but what you can do about it.

Focusing by Eugene T. Gendlin (Bantam Books, 1981) offers a simple technique you can learn by yourself for getting in touch with bodily sensations and unstuck from painful thoughts and emotions.

GENERAL ADVICE

A great resource is www.Soundwise.com, billed as Your Ultimate Survival Guide to Today's Tough Times. Join for free and you can receive free audio content on topics from surviving stress to earning extra income and layoff-proofing yourself.

GRATITUDE

My books *Attitudes of Gratitude* (Conari Press, 1999), *A Grateful Heart* (Conari Press, 1994), and *Giving Thanks* (Conari Press, 2007) explore the spiritual, emotional, and physical benefits of gratefulness, and offer many ways to practice.

www.gratefulness.org is a wonderful gratitude website created around Br. David Steindl-Rast that offers lots of gratitude resources.

INSPIRATION

When you're feeling defeated or hopeless, go to www.guzer.com/videos/are-you-going-to-finish-strong.php for a little uplift. You can finish strong.

INTENTION

Want help in keeping true to your intentions? Check out www.intent.com, where you can post your intentions and connect to others who are living intentionally.

MEDITATION

Go to www.tricycle.com to search for a meditation center near you. It's under "find a dharma center."

The Mindful Awareness Research Center at UCLA, founded by Daniel Siegel (http://marc.ucla.edu/body .cfm?id=22) offers audio instructions for a variety of meditations that you can play on your computer or download to an MP3 player. They include a five-minute Breathing meditation and a seven-minute Working with Difficulties meditation that you might find particularly useful. They also offer a couple of versions of the Loving Kindness meditation.

NEUROSCIENCE

If you would like to understand more deeply the neuroscience underpinning this book, a great resource is *Train Your Mind, Change Your Brain* by Sharon Begley (Ballantine Books, 2007).

www.wisebrain.org offers information, articles, and techniques from the intersection of neuroscience, psychology, and Buddhism.

PURPOSE

I Will Not Die an Unlived Life by Dawna Markova (Conari Press, 2000) offers the best perspective on finding purpose and passion that I have seen.

SELF-CONFIDENCE

My book *Trusting Yourself* (Broadway Books, 2004) gives dozens of ways to access your own wisdom and to grow your self-awareness, self-confidence, and self-reliance.

STRESS

Joan Borysenko is a medical expert who writes extensively on the mind-body connection. Her new book, *Stress Less* (Hay House, 2009), can offer real comfort.

TALENTS

If you want to learn more about your thinking talents, check out PTP's www.ptp-partners.com. You can buy a set of Thinking Talent cards to assess your talents, maps to plot them on the Domains of Competence, and manuals that can help you develop and use them more.

For Personal Support from Me

If you or your organization is going through changes, either those that were initiated or those you didn't ask for, I can help by offering the following:

- Thinking partnerships: Using a strength-based approach, I and my colleagues at Professional Thinking Partners can help you reach your professional and personal goals.

- Speaker and Workshop Presenter: I offer a variety of customized presentations that will benefit your organization.

- Change Masters Tele-Community: An interactive tele-conversation with me and other thought leaders every month along with other resources to help anyone going through change.

- Tip of the Week: Hear directly from me every week—weekly inspiration and guidance sraight to your in-box.

To contact me and learn more, visit my website at www.MJ-Ryan.com or check out my Twitter profile at www.Twitter.com/MJRyan.

Just for visiting my site, I will e-mail you a special gift of my Change Survival Kit.

WHAT PEOPLE ARE SAYING

"As an executive coach, M.J. has helped me perform consistently better than I ever have in my career. . . . In this very tough business climate, there are few people I can rely on with 100 percent confidence. M.J. is one of them."

—**Patrick Burke,** Hewitt Associates

"M.J. has had a profound effect on my life. I am so grateful for her help and wise advice."   —**Esalen** workshop participant

"M. J. Ryan was one of the best and most inspiring speakers I've seen in a long while. . . . I'd highly recommend her to any organization implementing changes that require a change of cultural habit. M.J. will help your teams create new results-focused habits!"

—**Karen Del Vescovo,** business operations and
marketing officer, Microsoft

Acknowledgments

In this book, I spoke about the need for partners as we navigate the waters of change. *AdaptAbility* would not exist but for a variety of partners I have been gifted with: Esther Laspisa has been after me for years to write this book and provided crucial framing conversations and lots of examples at just the right times. She's the godmother of this book. Dawna Markova's thinking informs virtually every word on these pages. Her generosity of spirit and steadfast commitment to our collaboration continues to humble and amaze me. Debra Goldstein of The Creative Culture kept the faith for almost two years as we thrashed out what book I should do to follow up *This Year I Will. . . .* She read every word, provided many examples, and went far beyond the call of agent duty in helping this book see the light of day. The rest of her team at The Creative Culture deserves a shout-out too, particularly Mary Ann Naples, who endured endless "What about this title?" conversations, and Laura Nolan, goddess of foreign rights. Change Masters Mary Beth Sammons, Allison Tabor, Beatrice Stonebanks, Catarina Vaticano, Stephanie Ryan, Annette Madden, and Kathleen Scott allowed me to pick their brains and share their secrets. Angie McArthur provided all the graphics for the book, which I would have been incapable of doing myself. Her quiet "can do–ness" is a great comfort. My clients offer a living laboratory on AdaptAbility. It's an honor to accompany them as they grow and change. Kris Puopolo at

Broadway continues to believe in me and my work and to make it better with her sharp mind. In turn, she's part of a team including Stephanie Bowen, David Drake, Caroline Sill, and Catherine Pollock who each do their part of publishing magic. Leslie Rossman and Emily Miles of Open Book have been my publicists for more than fifteen years. Their expertise is something I continue to count on. Thanks to Kenneth Gillett of Target Marketing for getting me out there on the Web even more. Last but not least, Donald McIlraith took up the household slack, including taking our daughter, Ana Li, away for Thanksgiving weekend, so that I could do this book on a very tight deadline. He truly deserves the title of Mr. AdaptAbility.

About the Author

Dubbed "an expert in human fulfillment and change," M. J. Ryan is one of the creators of the *New York Times* best-selling *Random Acts of Kindness* series and the author of *This Year I Will . . .* , *The Happiness Makeover*, *The Power of Patience*, *Trusting Yourself*, and *Attitudes of Gratitude*, among other titles. A member of Professional Thinking Partners, she specializes in coaching individuals and teams around the world. She has appeared on the *Today* show and CNN, and is a contributing editor to *Good Housekeeping* and *Health*. She lives in the San Francisco Bay Area with her husband and daughter. Visit her website at **www.mj-ryan.com**.